Hidden Restaurants
NORTHERN CALIFORNIA

by Anne & David Yeadon
and the Camaro editors

Camaro Publishing Co.
LOS ANGELES–SAN FRANCISCO

ISBN 0-913290-04-1

For *SUSAN, MIKE and PAUL*

NORTHERN CALIFORNIA

Oregon

REGIONS

THE HIGH COUNTRY

THE CENTRAL VALLEY

Nevada

THE COAST

THE GOLD COUNTRY

SAN FRANCISCO FRINGE

CONTENTS

A GASTRONOMIC ODYSSEY

INTRODUCTION

Have you ever been out of town—heading some-place, camping or just out for a drive or a long bike ride—and wished you could find a place to eat that you knew you would really enjoy? A memorable meal that would not be ruined by outrageous prices.

It was a search for such places throughout Northern California that brought about this special guide book—featuring out-of-the way places serving good food at inflation-fighting prices.

When we began our search, our friends in San Francisco assured us that our success would probably be minimal and that we would quickly return to the city for good food. The restaurants and cafes that we found, however, have made them eat their words and, happily, change their minds. Our friends now know that there are many excellent restaurants throughout the state, in towns both large and small. You just have to know where to look.

THE SEARCH

It took an immense amount of work to bring about this book. For nine full months we zig-zagged across the northern half of the state—talking, eating, writing, sketching and driving endlessly. We visited just about every place worthy of the slightest consideration—some 800 in all.

We have tried to consider every taste and need. For the diner who likes to watch his budget, we found a number of restaurants serving excellent meals at astonishingly low cost. For the traveler who is just plain hungry, we found dining rooms serving substantial meals of gargantuan proportions. For those who demand gourmet fare, we found restaurants that rival the most renowned in San Francisco.

It wasn't an easy task to find outstanding traditional American cuisine in the larger cities, but we did find many in smaller towns such as Cedarville, Olema, Los Gatos, Little River and El Dorado. We also found restaurants that specialize in the exotic fare of Salvador, North China, Norway, Hungary and Bavaria.

We hope that the results of our explorations will make your own adventures in Northern California more satisfying and enjoyable. If you occasionally are willing to detour from the main thoroughfares, there are an amazing array of delights awaiting wherever you go. A nice bonus of searching for these "hidden" restaurants is the chance to see colorful parts of the state which otherwise might be overlooked.

What must be remembered about this guide is that it deals primarily with budget restaurants. With the exception of a few outstanding "splurge" establishments, most of the remaining 150 or so restaurants provide excellent dinners for $4.95 or less.

It is our opinion that we have listed herein the best restaurants to be found throughout Northern California, at least for this year. Any that we have missed will provide discoveries for later editions. We would love to compare notes with you; just clip the card in the back of the book.

We hope you enjoy our little guide, your travels throughout the state and especially your dining out.

Bon appetit.

A FEW NOTES

FINDING HIDDEN RESTAURANTS

In each town most of our time and energy was spent not eating, but finding out where the people who live there like to eat.

We tapped as many sources as we could find: local newspapers and their restaurant reviewers, local wine and food societies, local meat and produce distributors, chambers of commerce (useful but occasionally biased), local restaurateurs (naturally even more biased), liquor store owners, gas station managers and—most important—the local residents themselves. Somehow out of this rigorous filtering process came a short list which then formed the basis, but only the basis, of our actual testing.

Sniffing out hidden restaurants is great fun. Obviously, though, most people don't have the time to talk with as many people as we did, but with practice and a little luck you may find that a couple of questions asked of the right people could lead you to a totally unexpected and thoroughly enjoyable experience in dining out.

EVALUATION

Almost every enthusiastic restaurant hunter has his own pet "checklist" of good and bad features. We are no exception, and below is a list of some of the factors we used to evaluate each of the restaurants we tried. First, some good points we look out for:

- *Courteous, as opposed to groveling, service.*
- *Spotless silverware, glasses and china.*
- *Waiters and waitresses who are familiar with the menu and take an interest in your selections.*
- *Home-baked bread.*
- *Homemade soups, as opposed to the minimally doctored versions of familiar canned varieties.*
- *Any efforts made by the chef to develop a repertoire of individually created sauces.*
- *Steaks cooked exactly to order.*
- *Special dishes prepared on request.*

Now some points which can cause places to be rejected:

- *Salads containing one variety of lettuce, period.*
- *Canned or overcooked frozen vegetables (unforgivable in one of the richest agricultural states in the U.S.A.)*
- *Precooked food, heated in steam trays and slapped down any-old-way on the plate.*
- *Lack of a worthwhile choice of desserts.*
- *Red wine served chilled (unless requested) or white wine served warm.*
- *One-winery wine lists (an all-too-common feature).*
- *Rushed service.*
- *A lengthy wait for a table even though reservations have been made (a common ploy to keep high-profit bars active).*
- *Oppressively loud piped music.*

One word of advice: Don't hesitate to complain if the service or food does not come up to your expectations. A low-key discussion with the manager will never spoil your dinner or embarrass your guests, but it will certainly improve service at your table and indirectly help both the manager and other customers.

THAT DIFFICULT QUESTION OF TIPPING

We work by a simple rule. For exceptional service and food we tip 15%, for average conditions 10%, and if we consider the meal poorly prepared, over-priced and badly served—nothing. If this rule were adopted by more of our fellow restaurant hunters, managers and owners of sub-standard establishments would soon get the message (emphatically trans-mitted to them by disgruntled waitresses) and set about making the necessary improvements.

Many people feel that refusing to tip, no matter how bad the meal, would be taken by the waitress as a direct reflection on the quality of her service. This is not so. In most restaurants tips are pooled and shared between all members of the staff, usually including chefs and kitchen assistants. So a refusal to tip is a reflection on the restaurant as a whole and does not directly penalize any one person.

PAYING THE BILL

When restaurant hunting, especially in California's rural areas, we suggest you carry sufficient cash to pay the bill. It's not that we don't believe in credit cards and personal checks, but the lack of consistency with which these are accepted by restaurants is amazing and the results can be embarrassing.

However, if you insist that carrying cash is a thing of the past, we have tried to help you by indicating which cards, if any, are honored at each restaurant. We use the following abbreviations:

AE	-	American Express
BA	-	BankAmericard
CB	-	Carte Blanche
DC	-	Diners Club
MC	-	Master Charge

This information was accurate as of the publi-cation date, but don't blame us if things change;

some managements seem to change their credit card allegiances from month to month!

LET'S HUNT TOGETHER

To maintain *Hidden Restaurants* as a useful guide, it will be revised at regular intervals. Prices accurate when this book was published will be reviewed, and restaurants which do not continue to hold the high standards we have set will be replaced with excellent restaurants yet to be found.

This is where we welcome your participation. Please notify us of any disappointments you may have experienced at our first-edition restaurants. Let us know of significant price changes and—most useful of all—tell us about any restaurants which you think might qualify for future editions of this book. We've provided a special form at the back of this book in hopes that we'll hear from you.

HONESTY IS THE ONLY POLICY

For the skeptical reader we emphasize that this book is not a series of advertisements. Reviews were carried out objectively, and each restaurant was evaluated against a long list of precise criteria. No one in any restaurant we visited ever knew we were doing research for this book until after the check was paid, and we accepted no free meals or similar offers.

In other words—it really is an honest book!

Anne & David Yeadon

NORTHERN CALIFORNIA

Oregon

Nevada

Occidental
Olema
Lagunitas
San Mateo
Menlo Park
Mountain View

Sebastopol
Sonoma
Port Costa
Hayward
Palo Alto
San Jose
Los Gatos

SAN FRANCISCO FRINGE

Unlike many other large cities, the fringe areas of the San Francisco Bay Area are distinctive in their own right, and neither the residents of the city nor the residents of the outlying communities wish the boundaries to be overlooked.

Many of our San Francisco friends assured us that, with the exception of a few restaurants in Sausalito, we would find the San Francisco fringe a gastronomic void. Much to our delight, we proved them wrong; and on the occasions when we invited those cynics to join us we took particular pleasure as they—almost literally—ate their words.

Those restaurants that serve unusual ethnic cuisines impressed all of us, particularly Mekong (Vietnamese) in Palo Alto, El Calderon (Salvadorean) in Mountain View, Tokaj (Hungarian) in Menlo Park, and The Pot Sticker (Mandarin and North Chinese) in San Mateo. And there was a fair share of just plain hearty food—at the amazing Banchero's in Hayward, the Union Hotel in Occidental and the Warehouse in Port Casta.

In the Splurge section we included a few unusually fine restaurants: Oscar's Bistro in Hayward, the Village Pub in Woodside, and Manka's in Inverness. We hope that you, too, will experience these treats.

15

BANCHERO'S

At 4:30 on an otherwise uneventful Wednesday in Hayward, Banchero's Italian restaurant was packed to overflowing. The crowd waiting in the foyer anxiously watched as the earlier diners stuffed themselves on a seven-course endurance test that would put many other family dinner houses to shame.

Our first suggestion is to get there early. Our second is to forget breakfast and lunch. Save all your energies for the spread here, which includes soup, salad and relish tray, pasta, entree, dessert and coffee—for as little as $2.50 a head. It's almost impossible to splurge in this place. Even the New York steak and abalone dinners (served on Fridays only) are less than $4.00, and if you're a pasta fan you can get away for as little as $1.75.

To be honest, we found a few rough edges. The service tended to be erratic; the over-worked waitresses had to scramble around with huge tureens of soup and enormous platters of fried chicken while squeezing sideways between the tables. And, on the day we visited, the broth soup lacked body and the chicken cacciatore ($2.95), although served in a splendidly rich sauce, was somewhat tough.

But there are redeeming features. The excellent tossed salad and relish tray, the garlic bread (50¢ extra) and the ravioli/spaghetti with an outstanding meat sauce, convinced us that this is an amazing place for the price.

- *Italian*
- *20102 Mission Boulevard, Hayward*
- *Tues. - Fri. 4:30 - 9, Sat. 4 - 9 & Sun. 1 - 9; closed Mon.*
- *Full bar*
- *No credit cards*
- *Reservations essential for five or more (415) 276-7355*

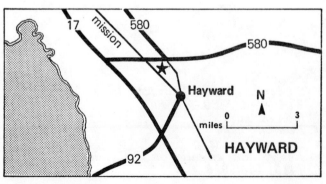

OLD VIKING

We once spent a long, lazy summer in Scandinavia, and our visit to the Old Viking here brought back memories of that trip.

The Old Viking is a splendid little place set back from the highway in a somewhat rustic chalet. It's also very small, so reservations usually are necessary, especially during the summer.

Some of the dinners are expensive, but there's an adequate selection for around $4.00. Included are Slottstek Med Potetspannekaker (beef slices with potato pancakes), Kjottboller (delicious meatballs with lingonberries) and Swedish-style short ribs of beef. With the entree comes a selection of Scandanavian breads, herring salad or soup, celery roquefort and a choice of four desserts. (We suggest the Swedish apple cake.)

We also suggest you try The Old Viking when you're not in a hurry to eat and run. It's a leisurely place, and clock-watching patrons aren't particularly encouraged. So unwind and stay for a while.

- *Norwegian*
- *Sir Francis Drake Boulevard, Lagunitas*
- *Wed. - Sat. 5:30 - 10, Sun. 1 - 10; closed Mon. & Tues.*
- *Beer and wine*
- *No credit cards*
- *Reservations essential on weekends (415) 454-9928*

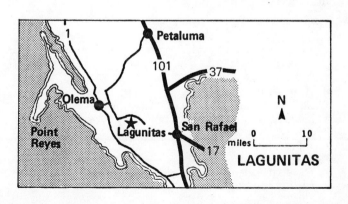

CRANBERRY HOUSE

Hidden behind the stores along Santa Cruz Avenue is an old Victorian house, painted a somber gray, which not only serves excellent traditional fare but also contains one of the finest collections of music boxes in the country. Columbia Records has produced two LP recordings from this collection.

Reed Whitelam, owner and creator of this unusual restaurant, somehow finds time away from the kitchen to repair and remodel his clocks and music boxes. If you display the least interest in his hobby, he'll give you an informal lecture on the glories and intricacies of the delicate little machines.

If, however, you are more interested in Reed's culinary prowess, try one of his fine dinners. They include baked crab casserole, steamed breast of chicken, red snapper filet and chicken livers saute. Dinners are served with soup, salad, dessert and coffee for around $5. In addition there is an excellent wine list.

And as if he didn't have enough to do, Reed also retails an extensive selection of his homemade breads, salad dressings, jams, chicken broth, pies and cakes.

- *American*
- *208 Bachman Avenue, Los Gatos*
- *Wed. - Sat. 11 - 2 & 5:30 - 9, Sun. Noon - 8 closed Mon. & Tues.*
- *Wine only*
- *BA*
- *Reservations advisable on weekends (408) 354-3162*

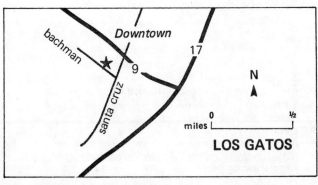

EL CALDERON

This tiny storefront restaurant, although located in a rather anonymous section of Mountain View, is amazingly popular. For lunch on Thursday or Friday, if you're not there before noon it's unlikely you'll get in. For weekend evenings, we strongly suggest you make reservations since the word is out about the good food here.

The menu contains a full range of Mexican dishes, but Roberto and Lita Lopez are particularly proud of their Salvadorean dishes, which have been featured in Sunset magazine.

We suggest you begin with pupusas—small tortillas stuffed with your choice of pork, cheese or beans, then move on to the main dishes. Particularly outstanding is the Pollo Encebollado, chicken in a rich sauce, for $3.75. As a side order, you might try the Frijoles con Crema y Platanos Fritos— fried bananas in a cream sauce with refried beans, for only $1.95.

Or you might try the rigorous Caldo de Res soup, a beef soup base with corn and slices of Salvadorean bananas (platanos), for $1.50. If you wish something truly authentic, there's Lengua en Salsa y Crema—beef tongue slices in a creamy rich sauce.

For dessert try the hojeulas—thin flour wafers in a light syrup.

- *Salvadorean and Mexican*
- *699 Calderon, Mountain View*
- *Mon. - Fri. 11 - 1:45 & 5 - 8:45; Sat. 11 - 8:45; closed Sun. & Holidays*
- *Beer*
- *No credit cards*
- *Reservations advisable on weekends (415) 967-9986*

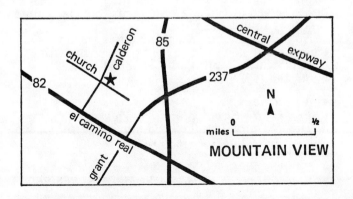

MEKONG RESTAURANT

During the last few years, Vietnamese restaurants have become a familiar sight in San Francisco. In the rest of the Bay Area, however, they are virtually non-existant—with the notable exception of the Mekong in downtown Mountain View.

This is the creation of Mr. Nguyen Ton Hoan, who back in 1964 was vice-premier of South Vietnam. Today, he is a proud host who delights in explaining the subtle blending of Chinese, Indian and French influences which characterize traditional Vietnamese cuisine.

Begin your meal here with an Imperial roll, similar in appearance to an egg roll but with a richer filling, in rice-paper casing. Follow that with one of the rice-based soups (we found the abalone and meat balls exceptional), and then move on to the entrees.

These fall into three main categories: sweet-sour, curry and barbecued. For beginners, we suggest the shrimp Mekong (deep-fried shrimp, vegetables and sweet-sour sauce), the beef curry (not hot, but extremely aromatic), or the pork a la brochette with barbecue sauce, all in the $2.50 to $3.95 range. Space won't allow us to explain all the fine differences between these and similar dishes served at Chinese restaurants, but be assured that they're not the same.

No Vietnamese dinner is complete without a banana beignet dessert—deep-fried banana with coconut sauce, topped with chopped peanuts. Fantastic!

- *Vietnamese*
- *288 Castro Street, Mountain View*
- *Tues. - Thurs. 11:30 - 2 & 5 - 9, Fri. 11:30 - 2 & 5 - 9:30, Sat. & Sun. 5 - 9; closed Mon.*
- *Beer and wine*
- *BA*
- *Reservations advisable weekends (415) 968-2604*

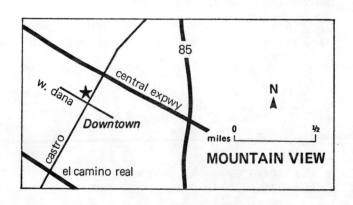

PEKING DUCK

The small town of Mountain View contains a disproportionate number of restaurants and even has its own Chinatown, around Castro and Villa streets. The tiny Peking Duck restaurant, with its bamboo-screened windows, appears at first glance to be one of the least significant Oriental establishments in the area. Even the very plain decor inside gives no indication that here is one of the most unusual and outstanding Chinese restaurants on the Peninsula.

As its name indicates, the Peking Duck specializes in Northern Chinese cuisine. The dishes tend to be extremely spicy, occasionally hot, and immediately distinguishable from the steamed and sometimes bland dishes which eminate from the Canton region.

We noted, gratefully, that there are no combination dinners. There are, however, many excellent dishes in the $3.00 to $4.00 range, including Imperial Chicken, Chunking Pork, Jade Fountain Shrimp and, our favorite, Mongolian Lamb.

Northern Chinese cuisine reflects Mongolian influences, and one of the Peking Duck's most impressive dishes is the Mongolian hot pot dinner. At $10, however, this was well beyond our budget. The same was true of the Peking Duck ($9 per person), which is served in the traditional manner—skin first, then meat fillets with thin pancakes, and so on until some fortunate guest is given the tail.

- *North Chinese*
- *702 Villa Street, Mountain View*
- *Wed., Thurs. & Sun 5:30 - 9; Fri. & Sat. 5:30 - 10; closed Mon. & Tues.*
- *Beer and wine*
- *AE, MC*
- *Reservations advisable, necessary for special dishes (415) 968-1040*

Peking

Duck

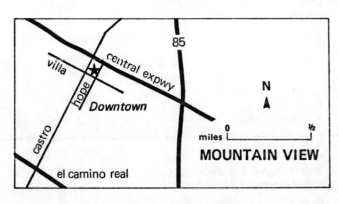

UNION HOTEL

Glowing and happy from our wine, we sat and plowed through an enormous seven-course Italian-style family dinner at the Union. To many Bay Area diners, the long-established Italian restaurants of Occidental are a renowned gastronomic fact of life. The very mention of the Union, Fiori's or Negri's elicits satisfied sighs or a booming chortle followed by long reminiscences of platters of duck and chicken and endless side dishes.

We are no exception. Whenever we have the chance, we will rattle on about our Union banquet of lentil soup, salami and cheese, salad, red beans, ravioli in a rich meat sauce, entree of a half a duck each with potato pancakes, peas and zucchini fritters, dessert of apple fritters and coffee—all for just over $4 each. If your budget is strained, try the chicken entree which is even lower in cost. Or if you want to splurge a little, there's a steak dinner for around $6. But if you're avoiding beef, stick with their lower-priced feasts—all very good.

Should you have to wait before you're seated in the dining room, visit the tavern. The hotel was built in 1876, and the bar dates back to then.

And should you not be able to make reservations at the Union (not unusual), try one of the other two Italian restaurants nearby—Fiori's or Negri's. They're both excellent alternatives.

- *Italian*
- *Main Street, Occidental*
- *Mon. - Sat. 2 - 9, Sun. 1 - 8*
- *Full bar*
- *AE, BA, MC*
- *Reservations necessary on weekends and during summer (707) 874-3662*

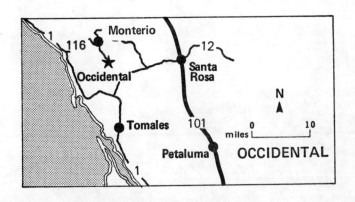

JERRY'S FARMHOUSE

The tiny community of Olema retains a flavor of turn-of-the-century Americana. From all accounts, the town once was a pretty wild place with nine saloons and a hotel of somewhat dubious reputation. Even during the lack-luster Prohibition years, Olema did a flourishing trade in "white lightening"; favored guests at Jerry's may have a tour of the old still behind the restaurant.

This isn't a fancy place, but the food is good, bold American fare. Whether you stick to the lower-priced seafood dishes such as oysters, sole or halibut ($4.00 to $4.50) or decide to splurge on the abalone or New York steak, you'll also be served soup, salad and a platter of freshly baked biscuits with homemade jam. A star of merit goes to the locally caught oysters, which are served pan-fried, raw, or in a superbly rich stew.

Lunches at Jerry's are outstanding as well as generous. Try the homemade chili with hot French bread ($1.20) or, for aphrodisiac-seekers, half a dozen raw oysters with French bread and cole slaw ($2.25).

- *American*
- *Sir Francis Drake & Route 1, Olema*
- *Tues. - Sun. Noon - 9:30; closed Mon.*
- *Full bar*
- *AE, BA, MC*
- *Reservations necessary on weekends (415) 663-1264*

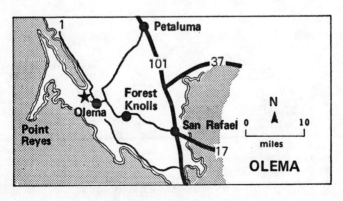

LE BISTRO

The cheerfully bustling Bistro, with its postered walls and red-and-white checked tablecloths, has long been a favorite with the student population in Palo Alto. And it's hardly surprising. Le Bistro proves that French restaurants need not be expensive to be good. Even with dinners in the $4 range, portions are generous and no corners are cut.

Of course, if you feel like something special, the management will willingly accommodate you with such delicacies as escargots (a half dozen for $2.50), Filet Mignon Princess ($5.25) and a rum cake dessert ($1.00). On the other hand, $4.95 will bring you a five-course dinner including soup, salad, rice or potatoes, fresh vegetables, French custard for dessert and coffee. Our favorites here are the Civet de Lapin (rabbit in red wine), and the outstanding Coq au Vin—both in the $5 range.

The wine and beverage list are both enticing and Le Bistro is an excellent, and reasonable, quality French cafe—a very rare find.

- *French*
- *463 California Avenue, Palo Alto*
- *Mon. - Thurs. 11 - 2 & 5:30 - 9:30, Fri. & Sat. 5:30 - 10; closed Sun.*
- *Beer and wine*
- *No credit cards*
- *No reservations taken (415) 328-3141*

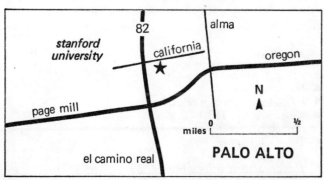

TOKAJ

If you missed a trip to Europe this year, a trip to Tokaj in Menlo Park will give you that good continental feeling.

Not to be missed on any trip to Europe would be authentic Hungarian goulash, and Tokaj's offers the most tantalizing we've found in the area. Not only is the goulash here particularly delightful with its rich sauce and light dumplings, but also the $4.95 price tag is less than you'd probably pay in Europe during inflationary times.

The second time we visited we tried other authentic Hungarian and Austrian dishes. Our waitress suggested fantanyeros as a suitable introduction to the fare. What arrived was a huge platter of rice and fried potatoes topped with breaded veal cutlet, pork chop, lamb and beef cuts, sausage and crisp paprika-coated bacon. Needless to say, we skipped dessert.

The entree is preceded by a choice of soup or salad (we recommend the soup) and is followed by a strudel dessert. You might try the palacsinta (Hungarian crepes) dessert, which we found exceptional. Tokaj also offers an unusually wide selection of German beers which blend well with the Zither music served up to you Thursday through Sunday nights.

- *Hungarian*
- *878 Santa Cruz Ave., Menlo Park*
- *Tues. - Fri. 11:30 - 2, 6 - 9,*
  Sat. & Sun. 6 - 9; closed Mon.
- *Beer and wine*
- *No credit cards*
- *Reservations advisable (415) 327-9583*

original home of Tokaj

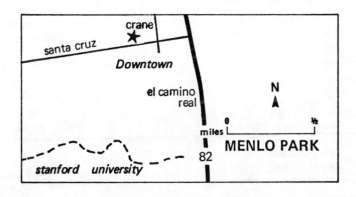

WAREHOUSE CAFE

When Bill Rich, an ex-beer-truck driver, decided to buy up the condemned and forgotten town of Port Costa in 1965, many heads shook sadly. He could more easily have thrown his money into the bay. Today those same heads still shake sadly, but with envy: Bill had found a gold mine.

Port Costa now is a fascinating community of antique stores, a fine hotel authentically refurbished by Bill's partner Jim Genereux, and two excellent restaurants—The Warehouse and the Bull Valley Inn.

The Warehouse resembles a film studio prop room, brimming with chandeliers, barbers' chairs, old popcorn machines, posters and washing machines. First-time guests often stand open-mouthed in awe as they take in this palace of potpourri.

As for the food, it's cheap, delicious, generous and beautifully prepared. Mondays through Thursdays, huge Basque-style dinners are served at a communal table for $2.50, including wine. The bread is homemade, the desserts unusual, and the wines are from the small Viano winery.

On Saturdays, Bill gives the kitchen over to an amateur gourmet chef, who offers his own specialty for $4.45. Then, once a month, on Fridays, it's show night—cabarets, plays, mime—for an extra $2.50 per person.

- *American/Basque*
- *5 Canyon Lake Drive, Port Costa*
- *Basque dinners Mon. - Thurs. 5:30, 7:00 & 8:30; Fri. - Sun. regular dinners till 9*
- *Full bar*
- *BA, MC*
- *Reservations advisable (415) 787-1827*

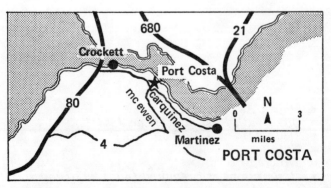

ORIGINAL JOE'S

The next time someone asks you whether you know the way to San Jose, do him a favor and direct him to Original Joe's as well. Joe's offers whatever you can think of in the way of food, from soups to omelets to sandwiches and salads—all huge and delicious. The food is farm fresh—especially the vegetables—and the quantities are gargantuan. Operating from the same location for twenty some years, Original Joe's serves what just might be the best food in San Jose—certainly in quantity if not quality as well.

Everything can be ordered a la carte, and for around $4 you can try top sirloin and eggs, meatballs with spaghetti and ravioli, pork chops, veal cutlets, calf liver and bacon, roasts of pork, beef or lamb, and baked ham. Any one of these will leave your tummy bulging.

Since Original Joe's is so popular with local residents you may have to wait awhile. If you're in a hurry, you may want to sit at the counter and watch the chefs perform their culinary feats. On the other hand, there's a cozy bar at the far end of the room where you can wait in a more relaxed atmosphere.

Original Joe's is unquestionably one of the special places in downtown San Jose—be sure to visit it on your way.

- *Italian/American*
- *301 South First Street, San Jose*
- *Daily 11 a.m. - 2:30 a.m.*
- *Full bar*
- *No credit cards*
- *Reservations not required (408) 292-7030*

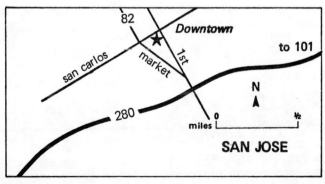

ELEGANT BIB

Have you been longing to dine in a place that makes you feel pampered and important, and at a price that's readily affordable? If so, a visit to the Elegant Bib is in order.

Decorated in a rich Victorian manner, this place puts a high value on the color red. If you are wearing anything that is red, be prepared for a pleasant surprise when you enter.

The remarkable thing about the Elegant Bib is that their complete dinner includes complimentary predinner cocktail, wine with your meal, and a cordial when you're finished eating. This makes the about $7 each price tag a real value.

The service is extremely courteous and every diner is given a free "Elegant Bib" (black and white instead of red) to wear while eating. Our favorite, which is also the most popular meal served, is their delicious rack of lamb. Strolling guitarists provide the musical background and, all in all, we left with the feeling that we had dined in a most remarkable restaurant.

- *American*
- *3201 Danville Blvd., Alamo*
- *Luncheon, Mon. - Fri. 11:30 - 2:30; Dinner, Mon. - Fri. 5:30 - 10, Sat. 5:30 - 11; closed Sun. except for Easter & Mother's Day.*
- *Full bar*
- *BA, DC, MC*
- *Reservations not required (415) 837-5123*

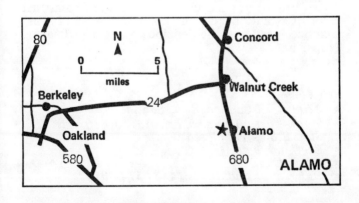

POT STICKER

If you're familiar with the Pot Sticker restaurant in downtown San Francisco (150 Waverly Place), drive down to San Mateo one evening and try the one on El Camino Real. The food is just as delicious but the pace a little slower; the first night we visited, it took over two hours to complete what we thought was a modest meal. The staff takes great care with the preparation of each dish, and dinners are normally served Mandarin style—one dish at a time—to provide a truly relaxing experience. Most dishes are in the $2.00 to $4.00 range.

For those unfamiliar with Northern Chinese cuisine and the spicy creations of the Szechwan region, there's a wealth of new experiences at this otherwise modest restaurant. We normally start with a plateful of pot stickers (steamed won ton-like delicacies fried quickly on one side only) and a large bowl of abalone soup. For the entrees, we select milder dishes first, followed by one of the Pot Sticker's hot Szechwan dishes.

In the first category we suggest the Velvet Chicken with Snow Peas (unbelievably tender), the Rolling Lettuce Chicken (a sort of do-it-yourself lettuce tortilla with a chicken, mushroom and waterchestnut filling), or the sizzling and sputtering Rice Shrimps (a great choice if you want to attract a lot of attention). On the hot side there's Prawns a la Szechwan and the delicious Mongolian Beef (super hot).

- *Chinese*
- *3708 S. El Camino Real, San Mateo*
- *Mon., Tues., Thurs. & Fri. 11:30 - 10, Sat. & Sun. 2:30 - 10; closed Wed.*
- *Beer and wine*
- *BA, MC*
- *Reservations advisable (415) 574-9910*

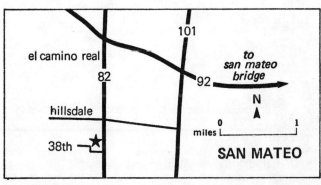

LE POMMIER

Le Pommier bulges at the seams on weekends. Be careful when you open the door: You'll find a swarm of people there, patiently waiting for a table. If no one gets crushed, it's well worth the wait.

Le Pommier is furnished very simply and is filled with the buzz of people talking and laughing together, giving it the warmth of a French home. Owners John Pierre Saulnier and his wife Josaine, who serve as chef and hostess, came from France only about five years ago. The rest of their staff is young and friendly, too.

In general, the food here is reasonably priced although you'll find a few splurge items as well. When we visited, the Special of the Day was fresh Rex Sole Meuniere, served with soup, salad, fresh vegetables and coffee for $3.95. There is an antipasto plate served with your choice of two soups, your choice of artichoke or tossed green salad, and homemade bread.

We also enjoyed the Boeuf Bourguignon in an exceptionally rich wine sauce—a huge portion for $3.95. Beef Tongue in hot sauce, Chicken Saute with white wine, tomatoes, onions and sweet peppers, and Fillet of Sole Veronique are some of the other dishes under $4.00. Also on the menu are steak and lobster dishes—perfectly delicious, but beyond our budget at $6.00 to $7.00.

- *French*
- *1015 Gravenstein Highway South, Sebastopol*
- *Tues. - Sat. 5 - 9:30; Sun. 5 - 9; closed Mon.*
- *Beer and wine*
- *BA, MC*
- *Reservations essential on weekends*
  (707) 823-9865

Le Pommier

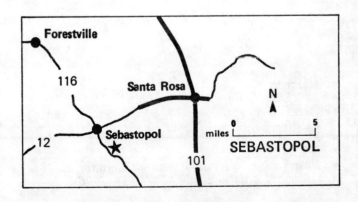

LA CASA

The wine valleys north of San Francisco are better known for their wine tasting rooms than their restaurants; however, if you fancy Mexican food, we recommend La Casa. It's just off the top end of the square and is directly across from the Sonoma Mission.

The first clue to the quality here is the tortilla dip. It's hot, bold and spicy, not bland like we've found at other Bay Area establishments. Also, for a change, there are some unusual starters on the menu, including an excellent sopa de queso (made with Chihuahua country cheese) and chimichanitas (thin tortillas wrapped around spiced beef and vegetables and deep-fried).

La Casa features a Combination Plate for $4.95, and offers a variety of other unusual dishes not found in all Mexican restaurants. And if you prefer such variety you can order a la carte, or if you're with a group, order Chinese style.

We found the chile relleno a little disappointing, but we recommend without reservation the beef and chicken enchiladas. Sea food lovers should try the Halibut a la Veracruzana, about $3.50.

- *Mexican*
- *127 East Spain Street, Sonoma*
- *Tues. - Fri. 11:30 - 2:30, 5 - 10; Sat. & Sun. 11:30 - 10; closed Mon.*
- *Full bar*
- *BA, MC*
- *Reservations advisable through summer, necessary on weekends (707) 996-3406*

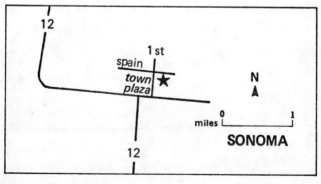

NORTHERN CALIFORNIA

Oregon

Nevada

Crescent City

Eureka

Garberville

Fort Bragg

Mendocino

Santa Cruz

Monterey

Carmel

Big Sur

THE COAST

The sight of the California coastline is always breathtaking, but the restaurants near the coast too often let us down. Poorly prepared seafood dishes were particularly disappointing, and several times we found leather-like abalone, overcooked and tasteless halibut or scallops with a texture like tough beef.

There are, of course, exceptions—notably in the Monterey/Carmel area where are found some of the finest restaurants in the state. To no surprise, most here are expensive, but it was here where we found The Clam Box, French Poodle and Consuelo's, where we enjoyed outstanding dinners at low cost.

We found noteworthy meals far to the north, too, at Lazio's and Samoa Cookhouse in Eureka, at the Harbor View Grotto in Crescent City, and at The Sea Gull in Mendocino.

BIG SUR INN

"All our visitors bring happiness, some by coming, some by going." That no-nonsense philosophy is the motto of the Big Sur Inn. It's a "come and get it or don't" pragmatism that extends to the practice of serving dinner at 6:30 or 8 sharp. If you haven't arrived by then, you won't be served.

If you do have the courtesy and good sense to arrive on time, however, the Inn is delightful. Warmed by a brick fireplace, the wood-paneled walls are adorned with such kitchenware as burnished copper pitchers and china platters, and the tables are set with brass candelabra and sprays of fresh flowers.

The entrees are limited to changing specialties each evening, and on the night we went we could choose between lamb chops, a vegetable plate, beef stew or baked ham. For around $6 the dinner includes a thick clam chowder, and a salad with homemade bleu cheese dressing.

The meal is ample and, though simply presented, it's well prepared. Four vegetables are served, and they're usually fresh. Apple, peach and boysenberry pies are available, but for some reason they're not always mentioned. Which is a shame since they're excellent.

Dinners are served by reservation only, and punctuality is a must.

- *American*
- *Castro Canyon, Big Sur*
- *Breakfast 8:30 - noon, lunch 12:30 - 3, dinner 6:30 or 8 (two sittings only)*
- *Wine only*
- *No credit cards*
- *Reservations essential (408) 667-2377*

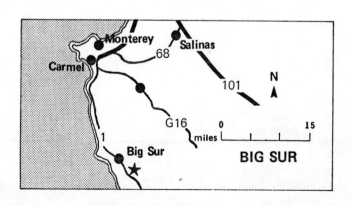

THE CLAM BOX

We tried The Clam Box on one of those cold and rainy nights when we had expected residents and tourists alike to be huddled in warm houses or hotel rooms. But that's the trouble with Carmel. The Clam Box was filled to capacity with hungry patrons, and we all but had to stand soaking in the rain outside waiting to get in.

A good reason for the extraordinary popularity is that this cozy restaurant serves excellent dinners at low prices. For $3.90 we could order a large plate of sand dabs served with a delicious homemade clam chowder, French bread, salad and a choice of rice, French fries or baked potato.

Other superlative entrees about $5 are a huge Captain's Plate (scallops, jumbo shrimp, oysters and abalone), steamed clams, Prawns Newburg, poached Monterey Bay salmon, curried Alaskan shrimp and Fillet of Sole Florentine. For a little over $5, the Crab Newburg ranks as the masterpiece of the house. The Clam Box also features meat and chicken entrees.

Seafood restaurants are plentiful in this area, to be sure. But among all of them, The Clam Box truly shines.

- *Seafood and American*
- *Mission & Fifth, Carmel*
- *Tues. - Sun. 4:30 - 9; closed Mon.*
- *Beer and wine*
- *No credit cards*
- *Reservations not required (408) 624-8597*

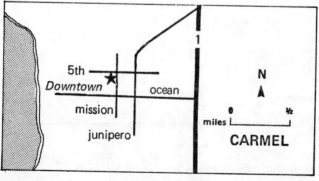

FRENCH POODLE

To enjoy this intimate Gallic restaurant, you first must call for a reservation. The French Poodle is filled to capacity nearly every night, and if you haven't reserved a table, owner/maitre d' Jean Becam will apologetically lead you out the door.

The cuisine here is superb. While every dish is a miniature miracle, we particularly recommend Les Ris de Veau Financierre (sweetbreads of veal, quenelles, mushrooms and olives in a rich aromatic sauce) or the exquisite Poulet Chaumiere (half a chicken in wine and port with mushrooms and truffles). Dinners here can be expensive, but more than half are reasonably priced at around $5.00.

If you feel extravagant, the menu includes a few tantalizing hors d'oeuvres, such as Escargots de Bourgogne, a delicious Pate Maison, and a Floating Island dessert, the house favorite. An extensive wine list is also available.

If you're in the mood for a quiet romantic dinner with candlelights, then the French Poodle is a must.

- *French*
- *Junipero & 5th Street, Carmel*
- *Mon. - Sat. 5:30 - 9:30; closed Sun.*
- *Wine only*
- *AE*
- *Reservations essential (408) 624-8643*

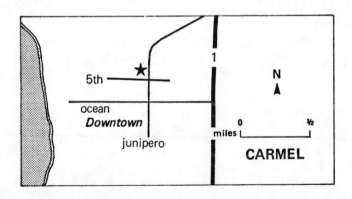

LA CASA ROSA

Looking at the world through rose-colored glasses has its advantages. You get to see the small, quiet, beautiful little towns that seemingly exist only in the eye of the artist. In these towns, obviously, you would also get to see old-fashioned, nostalgic pink homes that you might expect from rose-colored glasses. If this all sounds idyllic, it also sounds like a description of beautiful San Juan Bautista and its famous pink restaurant—La Casa Rosa.

And the scenery isn't all, since the best thing about La Casa Rosa is its food. Open only for lunch, they serve two entrees which allows them ample time to be prepared to perfection from original recipes. The chicken souffle is an excellent dish with a bread-like topping and the California casserole is a perfect blend of meat sauce and cheese. Each is served with a large salad of butter lettuce with herb dressing, and homemade rolls. Dessert and coffee are included in both these delicious luncheons, which are $3.50.

The structure itself was built in 1885 and has been a restaurant since 1935. The small perfectly cared for dining room makes you feel as if you're dining with the Shockey family—Jo, Beth, Charles and Linda, who carefully run the place. After lunch you can stroll in the beautifully tended herb garden in the backyard or taste any of their homemade jams, preserves, chutneys, or condiments.

The Shockeys' attention to detail and quality in both the decor and the food makes La Casa Rosa a place in which you'll feel as if you've returned home.

- *American*
- *107 Third St., San Juan Bautista*
- *Luncheon daily 11:30 - 3:30, closed Tues.*
- *Wine only*
- *BA, MC*
- *Reservations advised on weekends (408) 623-4563*

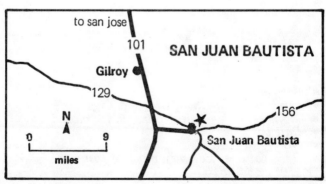

HARBOR VIEW GROTTO

Chub Howe, the portly owner of the Harbor View Grotto, delights in recounting how his restaurant remained intact during the terrible tidal wave disaster which wrecked much of Crescent City in 1964. It was the only building in the Citizens Dock area not to suffer extensive damage, and as builder and designer, Chub has every reason to feel proud.

He is equally proud of the food he serves. The prices are extremely reasonable, and the quality never varies—not even during the frantic summer months when the line of patrons stretches down the staircase and out into the parking lot.

Most dinners fall into the $4.00 to $6.00 range, and the selections include fried red snapper, prawns, fresh sole, oysters, fresh salmon in season, and grilled razor clams also seasonal. For the splurgers, Chub offers huge Pacific lobsters, steaks and prime ribs which run up to $9.

Of all the seafood restaurants in Crescent City, Harbor View Grotto is the one you shouldn't miss.

- *Seafood*
- *Citizens Dock Road, Crescent City*
- *Mon. & Wed. - Sun. Noon - 9:45; closed Tues.*
- *Full bar*
- *No credit cards*
- *Reservations necessary most of summer*
  (707) 464-3815

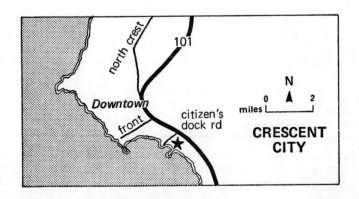

LAZIO'S

It's a crazy place—but a fish-eater's dream. From the outside it looks like any other dockside warehouse lunch counter, and it's no palace inside either. A huge glass-front refrigerator displaying the amazing variety of seafood takes up one side of the dining room, and that's all there is to the decor.

But the food at Lazio's is something else. Beginning with lunch (most dishes are in the $1.25 - $3.00 range), Lazio's offers a vast variety of seafood, from the superb Crab Cannelloni a la Portacella (crab crepe in a Mornay sauce) and bouillabaisse (served only on Fridays) to the more modest poached sole, crab and cheese sandwich and fried baby smelts.

The dinner menu is overwhelming, offering at least 100 choices of entrees. Eventually we selected Red Snapper Superb (in a rich, lemon butter sauce), Fillet of Petrale Sole (appropriately christened Filet Mignon of the Sea), and the Crab Chippino (a rich Sicilian stew), and each was less than $4.00. The dinners included a choice of Manhattan or Boston clam chowder, salad, sourdough bread, vegetables and beverage, and each is a masterpiece.

- *Seafood*
- *4 "C" Street, Eureka*
- *Mon. - Fri. 11 - 9:30; Sat. & Sun. 11 - 10*
- *Full bar*
- *AE, BA, CB, DC, MC*
- *No reservations taken (707) 442-2337*

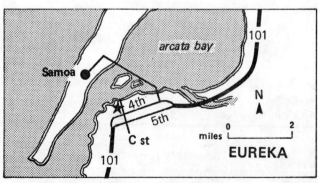

SAMOA COOKHOUSE

The town of Samoa is one of the last lumber-company towns in California. Around the turn of the century, almost every navigable dog-hole along this rocky coast had its little lumber community, complete with great timber bunkhouse and the inevitable and almost legendary cookhouse; now most have long disappeared.

Fortunately for the avaricious gourmands among us, the Samoa Cookhouse is no legend. Since it opened its doors to the public, this old lumbermen's restaurant has gained a notable reputation along the coast for well-prepared food served family style.

All meals, including breakfast and lunch, are remarkably hearty, but we especially recommend the dinners. For $4.25 you'll be served soup, relishes, salad, several side dishes including beans, two meat courses, vegetables, home-baked bread, homemade pie and a beverage. If you'd like more of any dish, you need only ask one of the bustling waitresses.

The decor of the Cookhouse reflects its lumber-town heritage. For an even better picture of how it was, artifacts from that era have been collected in a museum off to the side of the dining room.

- *American*
- *Off new Navy Base Road, Samoa*
- *Mon. - Sat. 6 - 2, 5 - 10, Sun. 6 a.m. - 10 p.m.*
- *No bar*
- *AE, BA, MC*
- *Reservations necessary for large groups only*
- *(707) 442-1659*

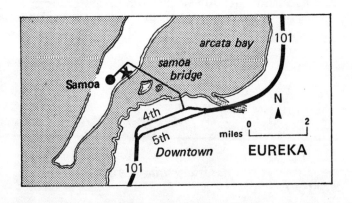

PIEDMONT HOTEL

For many years the Piedmont Hotel was a lumbermen's hotel complete with family-style dining room. Although open to the public even then, outsiders often were intimidated by the enormous bowls and platters served to the 'jacks and were embarrassed by their raucous antics.

Then the Ware family came along. Although the food is still as plentiful, there now at least is an air of calm and tranquility more appropriate to today's diner.

Although a few high-priced steak dinners are available, we feel the best values are in the lower-priced offerings—$3.50 to $4.50. The Chicken Saute Sec, for example, is a splendid dish prepared with white wine and buttered mushrooms; and the ravioli, flavored with a unique sage accent, is one of the specialties of Nobuko Ware, Jerry Ware's Japanese wife.

As with many restaurants along the coast, the local seafood dishes excel, particularly the sole, ling cod, and delicious fried salmon.

Dinners are served with a relish tray, a superb homemade vegetable soup, salad, coffee and dessert. And be warned: These dinners still are man-sized.

One last observation: Jerry's wine list offers an excellent selection of medium-priced California wines, a pleasant change from the more usual one-winery lists.

- *Seafood/American/Italian*
- *102 South Main Street, Fort Bragg*
- *Daily 5 - 9; Wed. lunch 11 - 2*
- *Full bar*
- *BA, MC*
- *Reservations necessary June - August*
  (707) 964-2410

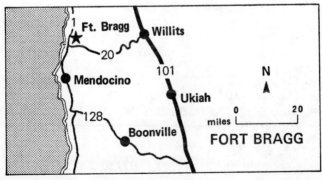

BENBOW INN

After many years in advertising, Arthur Stadler moved on to the restaurant business and created a stately, sophisticated restaurant in Garberville providing outstanding cuisine at amazingly low prices.

The huge Tudor-styled Benbow Inn could hardly be located in a more prominent spot. On a steep bluff above the meandering Eel River, its refined exterior peers down on nearby Highway 101.

To Art Stadler's credit, this hasn't turned into just another gaudy eatery, however. Over the years he's maintained consistently high standards with such dishes as Lobster Mornay (resplendent in a cheddar cheese and sherry sauce), Pork Chops Charcutier, Chicken Saute Benbow, Chicken Livers and Mushrooms, and an excellent Trout Amandine—all in the $4.50 to $6.00 range.

Dinners include an unusual variety of soups (we tried and loved the abalone), salad, homemade bread, beverage and a fine selection of desserts.

The spacious lounge, the Tudor dining room, the dining terrace overlooking the river, and an overall relaxed atmosphere combine to make the Benbow a truly pleasureful dining experience.

- *Continental*
- *Highway 101, Garberville*
- *Daily 7 - 11, 11:30 - 3, 5:30 - 9; closed completely Nov. 1 to April 1*
- *Full bar*
- *AE, BA, MC*
- *Reservations not needed (707) 923-2124*

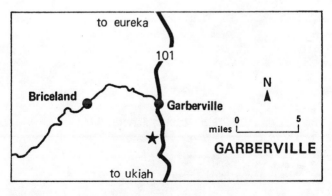

THE SEA GULL

What a joy of a place. Entering The Sea Gull is like walking into your own wild imagination. The little dining areas seem to drip with ornaments and antiques, including a stately bull's head, a ship's wheel, beer steins, unusual musical instruments, and ornate furniture.

Downstairs, in the cellar bar, it gets even wilder. There the flavor is Middle Eastern, and carpets hang from walls and cover the floors and the long, low settees. Groups chat quietly around hand-wrought brass tables while classical music echoes softly in the background.

Though the breakfast and lunch menus offer some interesting dishes (try the Japanese noodle soup for 95¢ and the mussels for two with French bread for $4.75), it is the dinner menu we found worthy of particular note. The relish tray includes such items as kelp, palm hearts, black grapes and pineapple chunks.

The entrees offer some excellent choices, including homemade chicken kiev, fresh oysters, calamari in Italian sauce, and the coastline favorites ling cod and red snapper. For a real treat, try the fresh Pacific salmon dinner for $6.50.

- *Seafood*
- *Lansing & Ukiah Streets, Mendocino*
- *Daily 8 a.m. - 9 p.m.*
- *Full bar*
- *No credit cards*
- *No reservations taken (707) 937-5204*

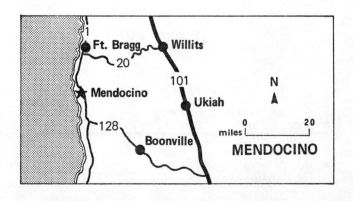

CONSUELO'S

A white Victorian gingerbread mansion in the Cannery Row area of Monterey is the home of Consuelo's, one of the most popular and attractive Mexican restaurants along this stretch of coast.

The decor is authentic turn-of-the-century chintz with velvet wallpaper, ornate, marble-based table lamps, crystal chandeliers, framed etchings and regal silk-sashed curtains. Definitely not the kind of place you'd expect to find enchiladas, rellenos and burritos.

Almost as soon as you're seated, a waitress brings a huge, crisp quesadilla topped with hot cheese. Follow it with one of the many combination dishes, all of which are around $3.00. For slightly more you can try one of the special dishes such as Sirloin Tips Mexicana, Carne Asada (broiled steak with guacamole, refried beans and tortillas), or the Fiesta Compuesta (a tostada with literally everything on it). We found the Carne Asada much to our liking—exceptionally good.

The only problem here is that the food and the atmosphere have attracted a band of ardent admirers who take over at 5:30. If you want a relaxing dinner, come before they do. But come!

- *Mexican*
- *361 Lighthouse, Monterey*
- *Mon. - Thurs. 11:30 - 9:30; Fri. & Sat. 11:30 - 10; Sun. Noon - 9:30*
- *Beer and wine*
- *BA, MC*
- *Reservations advisable (408) 372-8111*

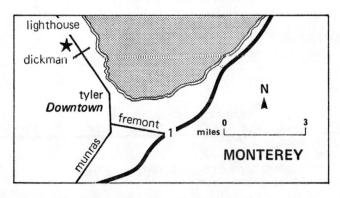

FUKI SUSHI

Fuki Sushi is an unassuming little place set back from the road in a particularly hodge-podge section of Monterey. But inside it's clean, crisp and fresh. The sushi bar sparkles with fresh fish and shellfish neatly laid out behind glass cases. The bar attendants (dressed traditionally in raised clogs, or getas) shout out greetings of "Irasshai!" to each entering customer while performing the act of sushi-making with great flair and skill.

One word of warning for the uninitiated: Don't expect huge portions of food in a Japanese restaurant. Although there is always a large ohitsu of rice presented with each meal here, satisfying your appetite is beside the point. To appreciate a meal here you should partake of each dish slowly and each mouthful leisurely; there are subtleties upon subtleties in this deceptively simple cuisine.

Most dinners are less than $4.00 and include shrimp and other tempura, steak teriyaki and salmon teriyaki. For a treat, try the Fuki Sushi Deluxe Dinner ($5.75), which includes three main dishes—assorted tempura, teriyaki beef, and a variety of raw fish served with soya sauce and green mustard. These are accompanied by a delightful crab salad, a delicate soup, endless mugs of hot Japanese tea, and dessert.

If you'd prefer just a snack, sit at the sushi bar and select dainty rice rolls wrapped in seaweed and adorned with a variety of raw fish.

This is an excellent little place for an unusual eating experience.

- *Japanese*
- *2339 Fremont Street, Monterey*
- *Tues. - Sun. 11:00 - 2 & 5:00 - 10; closed Mon.*
- *Beer and sake*
- *BA*
- *Reservations advisable on weekends*
  (408) 372-5440

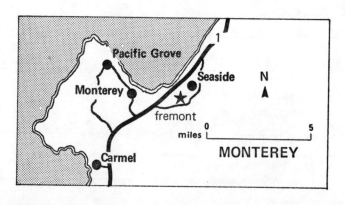

SANTA CRUZ HOTEL

This is an ordinary-looking place in a very ordinary sector of the downtown fringe. However, we were surprised the first time we tried to get in: the restaurant was packed, and we were warned of an hour's wait for a table.

We suggest that you make a reservation and also that you come with a big appetite and loose clothing. The cuisine is Italian-style family dinners, and the portions are generous and too luscious not to finish.

Be prepared for a generous relish tray, soup, salad, a plate of spaghetti and ravioli in a splendidly rich meat sauce, and a choice of entrees ranging from veal scaloppine, chicken cacciatora, salmon steak, and pot roast, for around $4.00, to the more expensive abalone and steak dishes.

- *Italian*
- *Locust & Cedar, Santa Cruz*
- *Mon., Wed. - Sat. 11:30 - 2, 4:30 - 9:45; Sun. Noon - 9:45; closed Tues.*
- *Full bar*
- *MC*
- *Reservations essential on weekends (408) 423-1152*

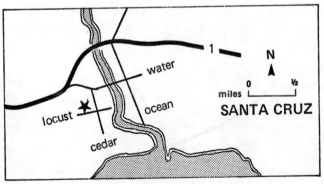

NORTHERN CALIFORNIA

Oregon

Nevada

Redding

Los Molinos

Corning

Chico Paradise

Yuba City

Sacramento

Stockton

Modesto

CENTRAL VALLEY

One might expect the flat, agricultural Central Valley to be devoid of notable eating places. Fortunately, that impression is incorrect, although we did find the search a little more grueling than usual. Also, we discovered that most worthy restaurants are located in the valley's larger cities. Sacramento is particularly blessed with excellent budget establishments, including the Hong Kong Cafe (an amazingly popular place on weekends) and the restrained Fuji's, which offers an unusually broad selection of Japanese dishes.

Stockton's Chinatown, while a little battered by continuing redevelopment projects, contains a wealth of restaurants, including the ultra-modern On Lock Sam's; the Villa Basque, one of the best bargain-eateries in the valley; and the unusual Olde Hoosier Inn, which has to be seen to be believed.

Out in the smaller communities, we found a true gourmet dinner at the NB restaurant in Los Molinos. And way up in Paradise, in the Sierra foothills, we enjoyed excellent fresh seafood at Pinocchio's. In the Splurge category, particularly impressive are the Woodbridge Feed & Fuel Co. in Woodbridge, Tony's in Marysville, and The Firehouse in Sacramento.

ITALIAN COTTAGE

With feet ankle-deep in mounds of sawdust and our mouths bulbous with crisp pizza and rich spaghetti, we passed a long-to-be-remembered lunch hour at the Italian Cottage in Chico. It's a rambling barn-like place with individual cubicles divided by wooden latticework.

Chintz curtains and red-and-white tablecloths add to the overall farmhouse atmosphere. While there are no ducks or chickens scurrying up a storm in the sawdust, the rush for tables at lunch time resembles a cattle stampede.

It's certainly not a gourmet dinner house. In fact, the restaurant's main claim to fame is the pizza: exceptionally crispy pastry with fillings flowing over the side. The hot dip sandwiches are an outstanding favorite, too, and include Italian meatball, pastrami, and beef dip onion with pepper cheese. In addition, there's ravioli and spaghetti with meatballs served with soup, salad, French bread, beverage and ice cream. Italian sandwiches are served in typical style, liberally laced with mortadella, galantina, salami, pepperoni or Swiss cheese. An ample meal can be had for well under $3.00.

Chico possesses few outstanding restaurants. (The locals will confirm this.) But the Italian Cottage restaurant, run by a charming couple, Bert and Judy Katz, is one reason to pay the town a visit. Also take a look behind the restaurant at Judy's pride and joy, the Things gift shop, which is full of local crafts.

- *Italian*
- *2234 Esplanade, Chico*
- *Mon. - Thurs. & Sun. 11 - 11, Fri. & Sat.
  11 - 1 a.m.*
- *Beer and wine*
- *No credit cards*
- *No reservations taken (916) 342-9607*

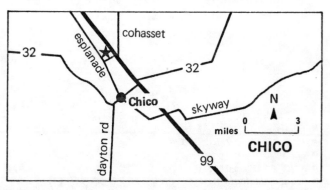

J & W CAFE

If you happen to be driving a diesel with a 50-foot load and you're wondering where the heck to park it, the J & W Cafe is an ideal stopover. Though a truck stop, you'll find an occasional camper or pocket-sized automobile hidden between the enormous highway giants.

This 24-hour diner is modern, clean and pleasant. A couple of tempting tasties are the homemade bread and the endless variety of homemade fruit pies which are served in double-sized portions and are guaranteed to give fastidious calorie-watchers a few palpitations.

The standard menu offers a goodly selection of breakfasts, most under $2.00. Meals of fillet of sole, halibut steak, prawns, chicken and veal cutlets, served with soup, salad or juice and dessert, are under $2.50. In addition, at least six a la carte specials are offered daily, including a masterful curried chicken, corned beef and cabbage, fish and chips, hot beef sandwich, and chopped sirloin. All specials are under $2.00.

This isn't the kind of place you'd go for cordon bleu cuisine. But if you happen to enjoy good, honest food served generously, backed up with chunks of fresh bread and slices of incredible pie, the J & W is an exceptional gastronomic haven.

- *American*
- *99W & South Avenue, Corning*
- *24 hours - 7 days a week*
- *No bar*
- *No credit cards*
- *Reservations not taken (916) 824-5484*

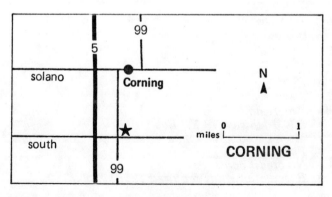

N-B RESTAURANT

Since 1949, the Nagos Brothers have been show-
ing the world how to run a consistently good all-
American restaurant. Moving to Los Molinos from
Chicago, they and their wives and children have
turned this insignificant-looking diner into a home-
away-from-home culinary gem.

Try starting the day with one of their breakfasts: a
thick, eight-ounce top sirloin, two eggs, a mound of
hashbrowns, toast and jelly. Tremendous! Dinners
at the NB are all well-prepared and superlow-priced.
Roast leg of pork, baked ham, veal cutlets, fried
chicken or filet of sole served with soup, salad and
coffee for under $3.00. The most expensive dish is
the top sirloin at around $4.00.

The Brothers' most revered creations are their
soups (at 45¢ a bowl) which vary each day and take
them hours of careful preparation. The Boston-style
clam chowder is perhaps the most popular, but the
split pea, chicken noodle, vegetable and navy bean
all are excellent.

At the rear of the restaurant is the Nagos Brothers'
well-hidden antique store. Teeming with clocks,
ornaments, crockery and other old goodies, the
shop is well worth a visit, although a purchase here
will cost more than any NB meal!

- *American*
- *500 Highway 99 E., Los Molinos*
- *Mon. - Wed., Fri. - Sun. 9:30 - 7:30; closed Thurs.*
- *Beer only*
- *No credit cards*
- *Reservations not required (916) 384-2310*

SINCE 1949

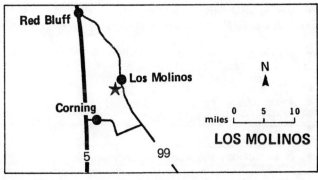

LOS MOLINOS

CARMEN'S

Located in a Modesto shopping center, Carmen's has boasted a fine reputation since opening 20 years ago. Owner Cip Duran and his son, Art, have managed to retain the authentic flavors of Mexican cuisine. Named after the owner's mother, and incorporating many of her recipes, this is one restaurant that refuses to pamper the often-gentle California palate.

Mexican food should be hot; otherwise it tends to take on a stodgy, sticky blandness, which we find unpalatable. At Carmen's, any dish other than the thick tamale is guaranteed to produce a healthy sweat.

The menu is extensive and offers sandwiches (try the delicious avocado and bacon), salads, tapatias, burritos, combination plates, specialties and American dishes. We particularly enjoyed Al's Special, a vast enchilada filled with chicken, rice, cheese, and onion, and topped with green chili sauce. If you want a real scorcher, try the Mexican steak, a thick steak fried with onion, tomatoes, and chili peppers, served with rice, refried beans (Carmen's taste richer than most Mexican restaurants), and a choice of tortillas. Prices are all around $3.00.

The combination plates are also a good value, particularly No. 4, which includes a cheese enchilada, chili relleno, guacamole taco, beans and rice for $3.50.

As Mexican restaurants go, Carmen's is a remarkably successful establishment featuring intimate booths and low lighting to complement their tasty food.

- *Mexican*
- *1700 McHenry Village, Modesto*
- *Mon. - Sat. 11 - 11, Sun. 4 - 11*
- *Full bar*
- *AE, BA, CB, DC, MC*
- *Reservations advisable on weekends*
  (209) 529-0208

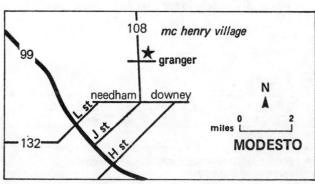

PINOCCHIO'S

A restaurant called Pinocchio's in a town called Paradise! Sounds like some land salesman's gimmick, but it's perfectly genuine. Marian and Jim Pinocchio, along with Jim's brother Frank, run this unusual, nautically flavored establishment at the top end of the city of Paradise.

The Pinocchios started in Hermosa Beach in 1950 and then opened another restaurant in Gardena before moving to the wooded Sierra hills, where they apparently intend to stay.

The decor of Pinocchio's would be more appropriate in a seaside location. Old anchors, ships' wheels, divers' helmets, models of famous sailing ships and porthole windows garnish the small dining areas. This "fishy" theme is carried through to the menu, which offers an excellent range of seafood: deep-fried king crab legs, swordfish steak, geoduck (huge king clams from the state of Washington), and a delicious mahi mahi. All are priced around $4 - $5 and are served with soup, salad, fresh vegetables and beverage.

Jim is particularly proud of his Italian dishes: lasagne, chicken cacciatori and rigatoni, all in the $3.50 to $4.50 range.

If you can manage only lunch, we suggest the huge char-burger: eight ounces of ground beef on toasted French bread, with fries or salad, for $1.50.

- *Seafood*
- *6929 Skyway, near Center Street, Paradise*
- *Mon. 11 - 9, Wed. - Thurs. 11 - 10, Fri. & Sat. 11 - 11, Sun 4 - 9; closed Tues.*
- *Full bar*
- *BA, MC*
- *Reservations necessary on weekends (916) 877-9571*

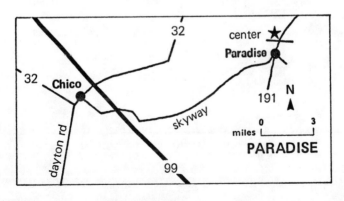

JACK'S GRILL

Everyone in Redding, including a meat distributor we spoke to there, says that Jack's Grill is the greatest place in town. The restaurant itself is just a downtown bar, which looks pretty ordinary from the outside. But the food is outstanding.

The menu, meals and prices are very simple. Dinners begin with salad, tossed in a dressing of your choice. This is followed by a selection of steak, seafood and chicken entrees. New York steak, filet mignon and top sirloin are in the $4.50 range, a good price for 14-ounce servings. Steak sandwiches, jumbo prawns, scallops and Southern-fried chicken are about $3.00.

The steaks, without exception, are delicious. The filet mignon especially, though appearing a bit lost on its oversized plate, was flavorful and tender. A baked potato and hot garlic bread are served with all dishes.

There are rumors that Redding's never tasted good food. After dinner at Jack's Grill, however, we can vouch that we've had some there.

- *American*
- *1743 California Street, Redding*
- *Mon. - Sat. 5 - 10:30; closed Sun.*
- *Full bar*
- *BA, MC*
- *Reservations not taken on weekends (916) 241-9705*

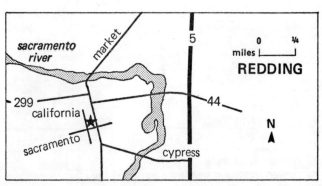

RAMONA'S

A busy bar opens out into spacious, red-carpeted, dimly lit dining rooms framed by individual cubicles. The only signs of Mexicana are the austere portraits of Spanish folk and the music which occasionally filters over the hubbub of the clientele. It's a smart place to spend an evening, although it's very much a family center. While sitting at the bar, your closest neighbor might well be a six-year-old pensively enjoying his Coke.

The menu is fairly standard. All the usual combinations and most of the dinners are under $2.50, with two exceptions. The Ramona Special—enchilada, taco, beef en mole, quesadilla, beans, rice, salad and coffee—at $3.25 is well worth the indulgence. And a healthy serving of the beef en mole is served with French fries and salad for just under $3.00. This beef stew, with thick spicy sauce and tender meat, is extremely rich in flavor.

The tacos at Ramona's also are especially tasty. Usually we fear for our precious tooth fillings, but here they're deep-fried and arrive puffy, golden and delicately crunchy, oozing with either beef or chicken.

- *Mexican*
- *Center and Trinity Streets, Redding*
- *Wed. - Sun. 4 - 11; closed Mon. & Tues.*
- *Full bar*
- *No credit cards*
- *Reservations essential (916) 241-0767*

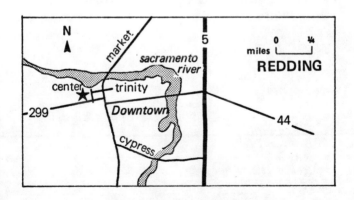

FUJI SUKIYAKI

Sacramento's Broadway Street isn't particularly imposing, and from the outside Fuji's restaurant is even less so. Inside, however, Fuji's is clean and fresh, and the Japanese cuisine is outstanding.

Even in California, Japanese restaurants are vastly underrated. American restaurant goers tend to be leery of raw fish, strange little spicy side dishes and steaming bowls of noodles in broth. As a result, trade tends to come mainly from the Japanese themselves.

The exceptions, of course, are those showpiece restaurants where the unusual experience of eating in tiny paper-walled cubicles and sitting without shoes around a low table often removes otherwise conservative inhibitions. Such places tend to charge for the atmosphere, whereas at Fuji's one pays only for the food—at amazingly reasonable prices.

For the cautious, there's the standard tempura/teriyaki-type dinners for around $4 - $5. The adventurous, however, should try the superb kaki dotenabe (oysters and assorted vegetables in soy bean paste), the tempura udon (prawns in a noodle broth), or the chanan-mushi (chicken, shrimp, mushrooms and vegetables in Japanese custard). All are unusual but excellent dishes from $2.00 to $3.00.

- *Japanese*
- *2422 13th Street, Sacramento*
- *Tues. - Fri. 11:30 - 10, Sat. & Sun. 4:30 - 10; closed Mon.*
- *Beer and wine*
- *BA, MC*
- *Reservations necessary on weekends (916) 446-4135*

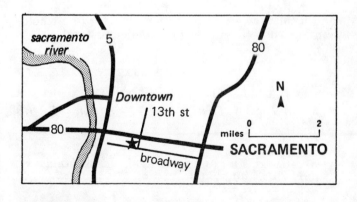

HONG KONG CAFE

This is the sort of place you probably wouldn't look at twice. Even once is questionable. It's one of the plainest, most non-descript restaurants we have visited. But it's also the place to indulge in some exceptionally fine Chinese cuisine.

The menu is simple and includes endless dishes of chow mein, chop suey (try the chicken giblets or peanut duck), noodles, egg foo yung, chicken concoctions and special dishes such as water chestnut chow yoke, ham yee yoke (salt fish meat), steamed fish, saute pork with preserved egg, and on and on. . . .

You only have to glance at the surrounding tables to realize that you needn't order many dishes to satisfy hunger pangs. The food is served in huge portions, and you'll probably find yourself with enough left over for the rest of the week.

The Sai Foo Oop—boneless, succulent, tender duck with bamboo shoots in a delicate sauce—is an outstanding dish. At $2.75, it's one of the few top-priced delicacies. The Hong Kong Low Special Chow Mein presents juicy strips of chicken, mushrooms and crispy vegetables atop a mound of tasty noodles and is one of the best bargains for the hungry diner.

This is quite a place. Well-dressed businessmen, long-haired students, chopstick-brandishing Chinese and local workers all blend together for one wholesome purpose: to devour this delicious food.

- *Chinese*
- *501 Broadway, Sacramento*
- *Mon., Tues. & Thurs. - Sat. 11 - 9; Sun. 11 - 8:30; closed Wed.*
- *No bar*
- *No credit cards*
- *Reservations necessary on weekends & holidays only (916) 442-7963*

樓港香

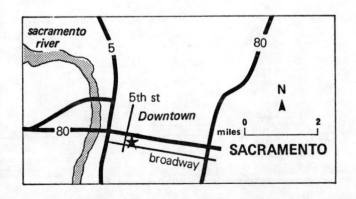

SAM'S RANCHO VILLA

You pay for your meal in the spacious foyer with its noisy waterfall before you enter the soft-lit cafeteria-like dining room. The focus of the dining room is the food counter, where enormous quantities of delectables are temptingly displayed in large copper chafing dishes and on huge silver platters.

Beginning at the far end of the counter, choose from a wide range of salad ingredients. Continue along to the prime rib (specialty of the house), turkey with dressing, and roast duck, served with mashed potatoes, spinach, pasta and gravies. Servings can be as big as you want, and you can keep returning for more and more. We advise that you take small portions, however; otherwise, the salad dressing tends to run into the gravy.

Beverages, hot rolls and desserts of ice cream and sherbet are served at your table by waitresses in elegant black and white dresses.

$4.35 for a cafeteria-style dinner may seem high. But, for as much prime rib as you can eat, who's complaining? For an even better bargain, try the $1.95 buffet lunch, which includes stuffed peppers, cabbage rolls, shrimp and rice and a salad bar.

- *American*
- *2380 Fair Oaks Boulevard, Sacramento*
- *Mon. - Sat. 11:30 - 3, 5 - 10; Sun. noon - 10*
- *Full bar*
- *BA, MC*
- *Reservations not required (916) 487-3464*

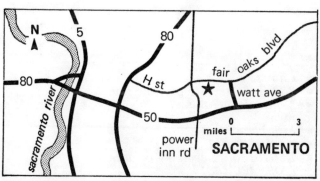

ON LOCK SAM

On Lock Sam's is a Stockton institution. There's been a restaurant of that name in town since 1898, although the original, located in an upstairs room in old Chinatown, was a far cry from the present. Today, On Lock Sam is a fine blend of strong contemporary features influenced by Oriental design.

Inside, it's warm and spacious. Tables look onto an enclosed rock garden, and booths are available for more intimate dining. The waiters at On Lock Sam's are some of the friendliest we have encountered in a Chinese restaurant. Show the least confusion over the extensive menu, and within seconds you'll receive a mini-lecture on Chinese cuisine with a mouth-watering explanation of how individual dishes are prepared. It's the kind of place where you can confidently leave the selection to the waiter—especially advantageous if you're with a group.

If you're determined to go it alone, however, we recommend the fried chicken wings, fried asparagus, curried beef, Chinese broccoli with barbecued pork, and, for the cautious, the excellent shrimp chow mein. If you stay away from the squab, lobster, crab and duck specialties, most dishes are less than $2.00 and worth every cent.

- *Chinese*
- *333 S. Sutter Street, Stockton*
- *Mon. - Fri. & Sun. 11:30 - 11, Sat. Noon - Midnight*
- *Full bar*
- *No credit cards*
- *Reservations necessary on weekends (209) 466-4561*

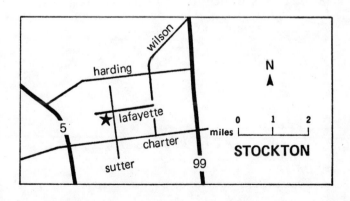

OSPITAL'S VILLA BASQUE

Most Basque restaurants in the Central Valley don't open for lunch; the frantic scramble of the 7 to 9 dinner rush is usually all they can handle. Ospitals, however, tucked away behind the crumbling blocks of Stockton's Chinatown, is a notable exception.

Lunch starts at 11:30, and within minutes the dining room is crowded with eager patrons fervently awaiting the first course of a midday bacchanal. Soup, salad, French bread, rice dish, entree, dessert and coffee—all for only $3.25.

How anyone can manage one of these lunches and then return to a productive afternoon's work is a mystery, especially when the soup and salad are served in help-yourself bowls and the delicious house wine is gratis. (Refills run a tempting $1.00 a bottle.)

Dinners, which run $3.95 to $6.50, are even more expansive: a huge plateful of ravioli or spaghetti, with side dishes of pigs' feet vinaigrette, oxtail stew, or shrimps with rice added as a glutton's bonus.

But don't assume the quantity of the food is all there is to rave about. Each dish is expertly prepared. Olive oil is used on the salad, and the main courses—which include beef bourguignonne, frogs' legs, veal scallopini and filet mignon—are all classic examples of fine cuisine.

- *Basque*
- *448 S. Hunter Street, Stockton*
- *Mon. - Sat. 11:30 - 2:30 & 5 - 10; closed Sun.*
- *Full bar*
- *BA*
- *Reservations advisable (209) 462-4377*

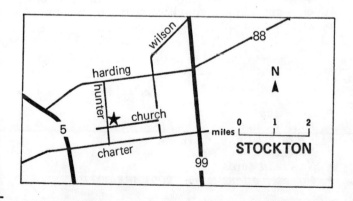

YE OLDE HOOSIER INN

Ye Olde Hoosier Inn appears to have been moved lock, stock and barrel from Disneyland. Pause awhile outside and read the inscription above the door: "Through this portal pass the world's finest people." A pleasant preparation for the pampering atmosphere within.

The Red Parlor waiting room almost defies description. Here we are taken back to Great-grandmother's days: marble-top tables, scrapbooks, Staffordshire dogs, velvet hats, Victoriana couches, tapestried chairs, fairy lamps, and numerous frillied dolls. The Victoriana theme continues beyond to the five colorful dining areas adorned with red regency wallpaper and wooden beams inscribed with verse. (Pick up the 10-cent booklet on "Thoughts To Live By." It's a gem!)

Having settled amidst all this splendor, enjoy the fine fare, which is wonderfully low-priced. How about a 10-ounce filet mignon for $4.95? Barbecued spareribs, roast turkey, jumbo prawns and veal cutlets are just a small sample of the dishes under $4.00. Evening specials run as little as $3.50. All dinners come complete with soup, salad, hot homemade rolls and dessert. The pies, unfortunately a la carte, are packed to bursting with fruit.

Hoosier's is an absolute must. The breakfasts, lunches and dinners are all great buys, and the setting—is something else!

- *American*
- *1537 Wilson Way, Stockton*
- *7 a.m. - 10 p.m. daily*
- *No bar*
- *No credit cards*
- *No reservations taken (209) 463-0271*

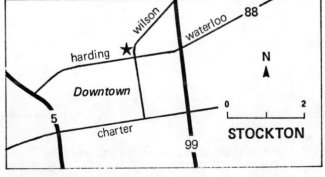

LEE'S CANTON

This restaurant has very few trimmings, but the color scheme is memorable: mustard yellow and red. Hardly sounds palatable for a dining backdrop, but somehow it works. The food is exceptional; maybe that's enough distraction.

If you're hungry, this is the place to come; the meals served here are usually enough for two. There are over one hundred dishes (we'd hate to be the chef here); if you should have any problems ordering, just read over the How to Order blurb at the front of the menu. It helps, and it's a thoughtful addition.

Our favorite dishes at Lee's are the special chow mein, the brandy fried chicken, and the black mushrooms and chicken. There are numerous chow meins, rice plates and chop sueys for the conservative diner. If you would rather sample American food, there is an all-around choice of steaks, veal, chops, ham and chicken—all for less than $5.00.

Lee's luncheon menu, ranging from $1.60 to $2.50, offers a new selection of over 20 entrees every day.

- *Chinese/American*
- *511 Reeves Avenue, Yuba City*
- *Mon. - Sun. 11 - 11*
- *Beer and wine*
- *No credit cards*
- *Reservations advisable on weekends*
  (916) 673-2970

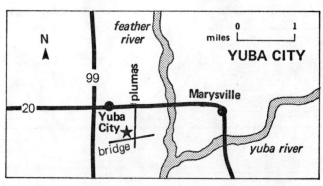

NORTHERN CALIFORNIA

Oregon

Nevada

Grass Valley • Cedar Ridge

Auburn • • Georgetown

Folsom • • El Dorado

Buena Vista • Jackson

THE GOLD COUNTRY

The Gold Rush Country of the Central Sierras
is rapidly becoming one of California's most
popular tourist sites. Fortunately, we visited the
Mother Lode Country during the early winter, so
we had a few weeks of tranquility in the wooded
foothills when we could meet local residents and
enjoy leisurely dinners in the evenings. The Molinas,
who live in Sutter Creek, were especially hospit-
able.

To date, the Mother Lode is practically free of
the plastic-plush restaurant franchises which are
proliferating as a gastronomic menace in other
parts of the state. Instead, we found excellent
dining in farmhouses, like Paul's Boarding House in
Buena Vista; in old mansions, such as Butterworth's
in Auburn (see the Splurge section) and the 1890
House in Grass Valley; and in old false-front buildings, like Poor Red's in El Dorado.

We found enormous family style dinners, at
Tarantino's Wheel Inn in Jackson, and even
outstanding Chinese cuisine, at the Dragon
Seed Inn in Cedar Ridge.

AUBURN HOTEL

Tastes change, but the Auburn Hotel will go on forever. The furnishings date it to the turn of the century, in fact it looks as if nothing has been touched since 1890!

We were served a six-course Basque/Italian dinner (family style) with a complimentary bottle of house wine. The meal began with a huge relish tray served with half a loaf of fresh sourdough bread, then thick minestrone soup, salad, pasta with beans, spinach souffle and corn, entree of fried chicken and roast beef—and a platter of cookies and coffee.

There is no choice of entree, but it changes every day depending upon the chef's whim. Among his repertoire are veal parmesan, spare-ribs, top sirloin steak, and the very popular Cornish pasties, a steak, potato and onion pie.

On Sundays there's a sheepherders breakfast from 10 to 2 which features fresh fried trout.

Residents of the town buy meal tickets here and regard the Auburn as a local institution. There aren't many frills, but the meals certainly are substantial.

- *Basque*
- *853 Lincoln Way, Auburn*
- *Mon. - Thurs. 6 - 10; Fri. & Sat. 6 - Midnight; Sun. 2 - 10*
- *Full bar*
- *No credit cards*
- *Reservations necessary (916) 885-8132*

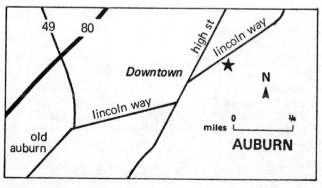

CAFE DELICIAS

There aren't many inexpensive restaurants in Auburn, but here is one that is gaining a reputation throughout the Mother Lode. The Cafe has changed locations a number of times, but we finally found it squeezed among an island of old buildings in the historical sector of the town.

We consider ourselves connoisseurs of Mexican food, but we've learned to beware of otherwise bland dishes smothered in dull, red sauce. At the Cafe, however, we were delighted to find that every item has a flavor of its own.

The chef has attempted to prepare each dish authentically; his pride and joy is the Steak Chicana—strips of sirloin steak prepared with green peppers, tomatoes and spices and served with rice, beans and tortillas.

There are 17 choices of combination plates—including burritos, tamales, tacos, enchiladas and rellenos, all served with beans and rice for $1.75 to $2.55. For dessert, try the Mexican Wedding Cake cookies for 20¢ each.

- *Mexican*
- *1591 Lincoln Way, Auburn*
- *Mon., Wed. - Sun. 11:30 - 9. ; closed Tues.*
  Closed two weeks in December
- *Beer only*
- *No credit cards*
- *No reservations taken (916) 885-2050*

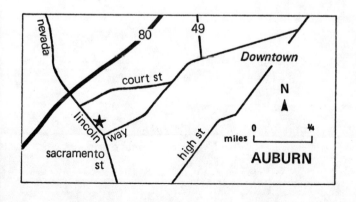

PAUL'S BOARDING HOUSE

Every weekend, Helen Kovacevich and her family and friends open their restaurant in an old farmhouse hidden away down a country lane surrounded by fields, fields and more fields. We got lost five times looking for it, but when we succeeded and then found how long we would have to wait for a table we wished it were even harder to find.

The meal is worth the wait, we assure you. On Sundays, it begins with a huge bowl of soup followed by a green salad, stacks of sourdough bread, ham slices, potato salad, roast beef and gravy, fried chicken, Helen's own ravioli, and the most delicious lemon meringue pie with coffee. All this for only $2.50.

On Saturdays, a superb stew replaces a couple of the other dishes, and the meal is just as fine, but even lower at only $2.00. The dinners are served family style and you can help yourself to as much as you think you can eat.

- American
- Camanche Park Road, Buena Vista
- Sat. 5 - 9; Sun. 1:30 - 9; closed during week
- Beer and wine
- No credit cards
- Reservations not taken

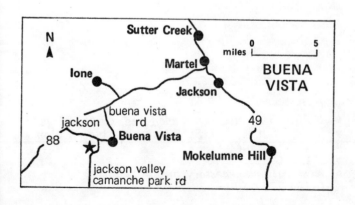

DRAGON SEED INN

We don't know how Joe Leong happened to open his Chinese restaurant way up in the forests around Cedar Ridge, but we can assure you that the food he serves would compare well to any oriental establishment in San Francisco.

Too often, combination plates can be disasters, but here they are superb. For just over $3.00, we were served egg flower soup, egg foo yung in oyster sauce, chow mein, spring roll and half a dozen deep-fried prawns.

The a la carte menu is limited, but it offers such dishes as Shrimp Rangoon (shrimp prepared with pea pods, bamboo shoots, water chestnuts and mushrooms), Prawns Tempura (a huge plateful), and an excellent Mandarin duck.

There also are American dishes uniquely prepared and well worth a try. Among them, we recommend the pork chops with apple sauce or the halibut steak, both under $3.50.

- *Chinese*
- *Colfax Hwy. at Brunswick Road, Cedar Ridge*
- *Tues. - Sat. 4 - 10; Sun. Noon - 9; closed Mon.*
- *Beer and wine*
- *BA, MC*
- *Reservations necessary on weekends*
  (916) 273-0520

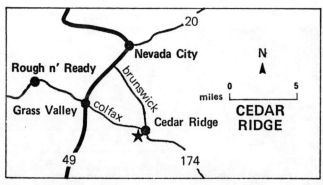

POOR RED'S

If you're here 30 minutes after Red opens the door, be prepared to meet half of Northern California. This is a busy, busy place, and it's not uncommon for guests to wait a couple of hours to be seated in the dining room.

We got the impression that Red's pre-inflation prices are what's keeping him poor. Last year he sold 41½ tons of spareribs, however, which ain't bad for a place serving less than a dozen small tables.

The barbecued ribs are under $3.00; they overlap the plate they're served on and they taste just great. If you enjoy the sauce, Red will sell you a gallon for $7.50.

Chicken is in the same $3.00 price range. The New York and filet steaks are a little more but still quite reasonable. A regular steak weighs in at 14 ounces, with a Special at 20 ounces. At lunchtime you can enjoy a 10-ounce New York steak sandwich with salad for less than $3.00.

If you push, signal or yell your drink order to the bartender, you're in for another surprise. Red's mixed cocktails are served in two glasses, and even those are overflowing.

- *American*
- *Main Street, El Dorado*
- *Mon. - Sat. 11:30 - 2, 5 - 11, Sun. 2 - 11*
- *Full bar*
- *MC*
- *No reservations taken (916) 622-2901*

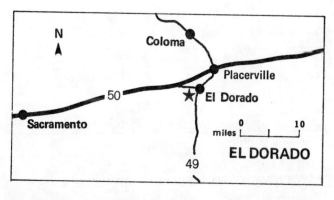

JOE & DODIES

Tuesdays are big nights at Joe & Dodies. Cars overflow the parking lot, and the street is one long chain of chrome and steel. Tuesday is Lobster Night, and patrons flock from as far as Reno to feast on 16- to 20-ounce Australian lobsters for about $9.50. This is one of the few splurges.

The event is becoming a Folsom tradition, and Thursdays are the same—when the repast centers on great slices of prime rib for around $5.00.

On Wednesdays and the rest of the week, Joe & Dodies can be counted on for a leisurely meal in the tiny dining room decorated with Tiffany-styled lamps. The specialty here is steaks, but the menu is extensive and there are dishes to suit every budget. For $3.50 to $4.50, we recommend the barbecued steak, the barbecued ribs, the combination seafood plate or the very generous prime rib sandwich. For another splurge, try the huge prime rib/lobster combination.

The lunch menu offers such dishes as a French dip sandwich, breaded veal cutlets, beef bits in mushroom sauce, and sirloin tips and noodles for around $2.00.

- *American*
- *13407 Folsom Boulevard, Folsom*
- *Daily Noon - 11*
- *Full bar*
- *BA, MC*
- *No reservations taken (916) 985-4050*

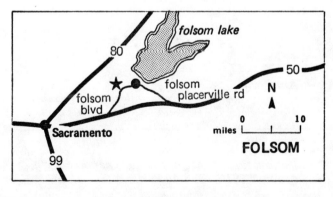

BUCKEYE LODGE

The Buckey Lodge is in the boondocks of the Mother Lode Country. People will tell you it's in Georgetown, but it's a good few miles of twisted road past there, high up in the evergreen foothills.

Chickens and ducks and other farmyard animals will be out to greet you, so be careful if you're traveling with a dog. (Please keep him away from the poultry, especially.) The farmhouse simplicity extends inside, too, where the feeling is that you've been welcomed into owners Robert and Blanche Cooper's home.

Dinners include relish plate, soup and salad and range from $4.00 for fried chicken, shrimp curry (flavorful but not much like Indian curry) and baked ham to $5.25 for Beef Brochettes Polynesian and $6.75 for a generous top sirloin. Meals also are offered a la carte, for 75¢ less.

- *American*
- *Country Road 63, three miles east of Georgetown*
- *Wed. - Sat. 5 - 10, Sun. 3 - 9; closed Mon. & Tues; closed Jan. - Mar.*
- *Full bar*
- *BA, MC*
- *Reservations necessary on weekends during summer (916) 333-4441*

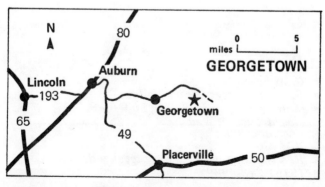

1890 HOUSE

We had all but declared Grass Valley void of restaurants to recommend when one of the locals asked whether we had been to the 1890 House. We tried it and felt as if we had struck gold.

The decor here is true Victoriana. Small rooms covered with trinkets, paintings, photographs and chandeliers—an interior decorator's nightmare but a restaurant hunter's dream.

Dinners begin with an excellent soup and a salad served with home-baked bread. The choice of entrees normally includes pork chops in cream, eggplant parmesan (both around $5.00) and New York steak, and the house specialities, chicken and lamb curries. Excellent!

For dessert, the pies are delicious and the coffee is about the finest we've tasted yet. In fact, if you're partial to a good cup of coffee, we would recommend 1890 House even for that feature alone.

- *Continental*
- *226 Mill Street, Grass Valley*
- *Mon., Thurs. - Sat. 6 - 10; Sun. 5 - 9; closed Tues. & Wed.*
- *Beer and wine*
- *BA, MC*
- *Reservations necessary on weekends (916) 273-5989*

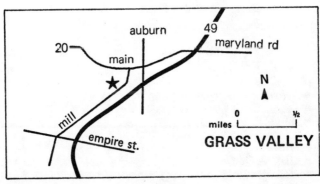

SCHEIDEL'S

Located in a wooden setting south of Grass Valley, this restaurant's exterior reflects Swiss chalet styling, but inside the decor is more restrained. And yet it provides a cozy continental feeling.

The menu features European and American selections and everything is made to order. From their long list of selections, be prepared to feast on one or more of their most popular dishes: Swiss rahmschnitzel, Austrian wienerschnitzel, German marinated sauerbraten, fresh trout, or rack of lamb for one. And if that's not enough they're also served with homemade Swiss pumpernickel bread, and a family style tureen of soup. Our favorite was the sauerbraten which we tried twice in one week.

The rainbow trouts served for dinner are displayed to you "live" in the aquarium in the lobby of the restaurant.

On the weekends you'll be serenaded by strolling Swiss accordian players and yodlers to complete the continental atmosphere. And after dinner you can blow the authentic Swiss alpenhorn located in the bar area.

Dinner prices at Scheidel's run from $3.50 to about $5.50.

- *German/Continental*
- *Alta Sierra Drive, Grass Valley*
- *Wed. - Sat. 4:30 - 10; Sun. 3 - 9;*
  closed Mon. & Tues.
- *Full bar*
- *BA, MC*
- *Reservations necessary on weekends (916) 273-5553*

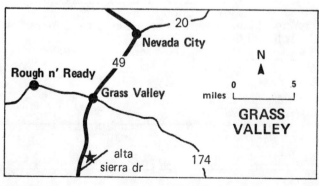

ROSSETTI'S

If you've wondered what ever happened to good old fashioned food values and old fashioned times, they are both alive and well, and thriving at Rossetti's.

Located on Hwy. 12 in Wallace (on the way to Angel's Camp), Rossetti's is practically the center of the community and is a perfect place to eat before starting an adventurous gold-panning weekend. It is a family-run place that has been in business for over 50 years, and for good reason.

When you enter, be prepared to hear cheerful piano music, see local friends boisterously talking, and be greeted as if your presence will make the night even more special. Buck was our host the last time we visited and he just couldn't wait to introduce us to Geno and his family, the people who have run Rossetti's since the beginning.

The seating arrangement consists of small, nicely aged tables in each of the two dining areas, and the food is—well—it's just plain good food. Operated very much like a community dinner with fast and friendly waitresses, the food is mostly a staple fare with Italian overtones. We tried the fried chicken and the gulf prawns which included a relish tray, a tureen of soup, salad, pasta, entree, dessert, and coffee and all for only $4.95 each!

If you'd like to try a touch of the rural country-side along with some good home-style cooking then don't miss Rossetti's—there aren't too many places like this left.

- *American/Italian*
- *Hwy. 12, Wallace*
- *Wed. - Sun. 5:30 - 9:30; closed Mon. & Tues.*
- *Full bar*
- *No credit cards*
- *Reservations not needed (209) 763-5130*

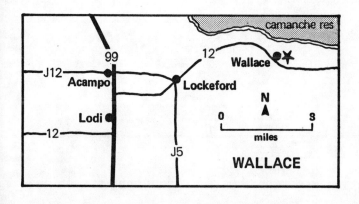

WHEEL INN

Whether you're headed for Tarantino's or the Wheel Inn, it matters not for they're one and the same. We had thought it coincidental that the two buildings are next to each other and that both advertise Italian food; looking for Tarantino's, however, we found the entrance where the sign says Wheel Inn. It's confusing only once.

The meal begins with a relish tray followed by a huge bowl of soup, salad, two pasta dishes and a basket of fresh French bread. Go easy because the entrees are enormous; the veal scaloppine is nearly the size of the platter it's served on. Other dishes outstanding in both taste and quantity are Veal Piccata (veal with lemon and mushrooms), Veal Parmigiana, halibut steak, roast chicken, fillet of sole and pork chops; all are around $4.00.

For a little more, Tarantino's Wheel Inn occasionally offers a superb rack of lamb. We tried it with a fine D'Agostini Zinfandel (a splendid wine produced locally) and we rate it one of our exceptional experiences in the Mother Lode.

- *Italian*
- *1106 Jackson Gate Rd.*
- *Tues. - Fri. 5 - 10; Sat. 5 - 11 & Sun. 1 - 9; closed Mon.*
- *Full bar*
- *BA, MC*
- *Reservations advisable (209) 223-1008*

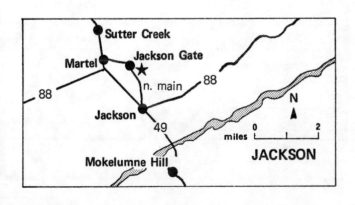

NORTHERN CALIFORNIA

Oregon

Alturas • • Cedarville

• Susanville

Chester •

Reno • Nevada
• Sparks
Tahoe City •
• Gardnerville

Mammoth Lakes •

THE HIGH COUNTRY

People in the bleak, rugged high country are known for their appetites. As one old farmer told us in the market town of Alturas, "Ain't nuthin' much to do 'cept eat." Restaurants, although scattered throughout the region, cater mainly to the local residents, who care not so much about the quality of cuisine as about the volume of food and the number of courses.

Places like Golden's, tucked away at the northeastern border in Surprise Valley, and the Mt. Lassen Club, in the sturdy little town of Chester, are typical of the region. There's no nonsense here: The decor is plain, the service is casual but friendly, and the food is surprisingly good.

In contrast, we slipped over the border into Reno and found Eugene's (see the Splurge section), an outstanding restaurant with a fine selection of classic continental dishes. We found other fine settings and menus at the Timber House in Chester and The Hearthstone in Tahoe City. These cater to the seasonal tourist trade, and the atmosphere appeals particularly to a cosmopolitan clientele.

RANCHO STEAK HOUSE

Don Gillespie, a furniture manufacturer from Los Angeles, took over the Rancho Steak House three years ago. He had thought that moving to Alturas would allow him to live that little bit longer.

However, the life of ease and the semi-retirement that Don expected doesn't seem to be working out. On the night we visited, the restaurant was about to receive a face lift: new furnishings, new bar, new drapes. The redecorating had been inspired by the restaurant's tremendous popularity in an area not known for fine dining establishments; Don may have to look elsewhere for his life of ease.

Despite it being on the main Redding highway (299), the restaurant is a quiet place to appreciate a meal. Most dinners are priced under $4.00; the 18-ounce New York steak, at $5.50, is one of the few exceptions, but no steak served here is under 16-ounces. The ground sirloin with mushroom gravy and baked potato, for $2.75, is a bargain.

Other dishes include salmon steak, sole, halibut, jumbo shrimp and a combination seafood plate. All dinners are served with French bread and a baked potato with individual bowls of butter, sour cream and chives. Salads and sandwiches also are offered.

The piece de resistance of this homey yet smart restaurant is the salad bar. Although simply displayed, at least 12 salads are available, and the number of times you visit the bar seems to be of little concern to Don.

- *American*
- *Redding Highway 299, Alturas*
- *Mon. - Sat. 12 to 10; closed Sun.*
- *Full bar*
- *BA, MC*
- *Reservations advisable (916) 233-2529*

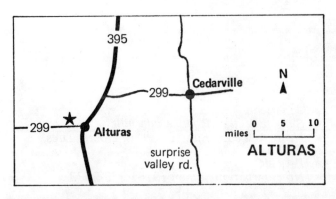

GOLDEN'S

Imagine a hidden corner of California, a tiny town full of false-front, turn-of-the-century architecture, eagles circling slowly around snow-topped mountain peaks, woods populated with deer, porcupines and raccoons, and brilliant sunsets reflected in still lakes. That's Surprise Valley, way up in the northeastern corner of the state.

Golden's Restaurant is the only eating place in the area, located opposite an old two-story brick store in the community of Cedarville.

The bar adjoining the dining room at Golden's is the social center of the town. Every night it's packed with vociferous locals who boldly hurl greetings at one another and dance around the juke box as if tomorrow would never come.

By contrast, the dining room is quiet. Dinners, served by pretty, red-cheeked waitresses, consist of a generous relish tray, a tureen of thick, home-made soup, and your choice of veal in mushroom sauce, chef's steak, fried chicken or prawns, with garlic bread, onion rings, spaghetti and vegetables. Dessert and coffee are included.

Most meals are around $4.00, but there's a 14-ounce top sirloin at $6.00 for the extravagant. If you're lucky, you might be offered the superb prime rib special at $3.85.

- *American*
- *Surpise Valley Road, Cedarville*
- *Mon. & Wed. - Sun. 6 - 9:30; closed Tues.*
- *Full bar*
- *BA, MC*
- *No reservations taken (916) 279-2333*

MODOC BRANDS

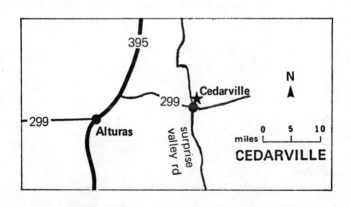

MT. LASSEN CLUB

The local postmistress, Maude Gay, built the Mt. Lassen Club quite a few years ago as a warehouse. Today the warehouse is experiencing amazing popularity as an outstanding dining establishment. The decor is nothing to rave about and from the outside it still looks like a warehouse. But the food and the hospitality here are memorable.

Meals begin with the largest of relish trays, including a variety of fresh vegetables and a tasty dip. The tossed green salad is served with garlic bread, but take it easy: the best is yet to come.

A 16-ounce rainbow trout, an 11-ounce top sirloin steak or an unforgettable pile of barbecued spareribs are just a sample of the dishes served at the Club for under $4.00. If you should have an insatiable appetite, there is a 32-ounce T-bone steak, a 16-ounce filet mignon or a 18-ounce New York steak, all in the $6.00 to $7.00 range but worth every cent. As you may gather, the menu is small but the food is outstanding and plentiful.

The Mt. Lassen Club is no palace. Diners, gorging their way through vast platters of steak, do so accompanied by the juke box or local maestros banging on the honky-tonk piano. If you enjoy a raucous bar atmosphere as well as great food, however, you'll love it here.

- Steaks
- Main Street, Chester
- Daily 4 - about 9:30
- Full bar
- No credit cards
- No reservations taken (916) 258-9901

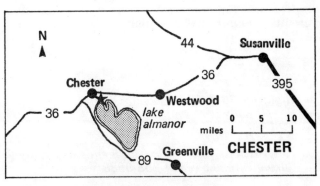

TIMBER HOUSE LODGE

Sam Herreld was quite a man. Many of his neighbors thought him a bit crazy when he started building his Timber House single-handedly, but when they finally saw the results of his four years of back-breaking effort, Sam instantly became a local legend.

The Timber House is an amazing building. Inside, the design tends to suggest a crude Polynesian decor, with hollowed-out tree trunks used as chandeliers, a huge hand-hewn bar, tables roughly fashioned from timber which Sam dragged from nearby forests, a massive 300-pound door and 18-inch-thick wooden walls.

Today, Sam's Timber House is owned by Jim and Gena Hupp, who have turned it into one of Chester's better restaurants. Most of the dinners are under $4.50. The delightful chicken breast cordon bleu stuffed with imported ham and Swiss cheese, the chicken a la maison (boneless breast of chicken stuffed with apples, almonds and bread dressing), sweet and sour spareribs, a small top sirloin steak, brochette of beef on rice pilaf, rainbow trout, and grilled halibut steak are just a few excellent dishes from the varied menu. Dinners are preceded by a relish plate, a green salad and hot, toasted cheese bread.

The Lodge provides an intimate, comfortable and unusual setting for a drink at the bar, a cup of coffee or a full dinner. Whatever you decide on, credit to Sam Herreld is due.

- *American*
- *Highway 36 & First Street, Chester*
- *8 - 10 daily*
- *Full bar*
- *BA, MC*
- *Reservations essential on weekends and daily during summer (916) 258-9989*

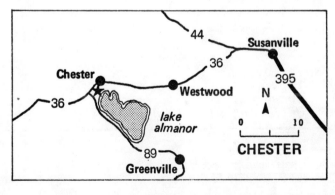

J. T. BASQUE

At one time a blacksmith's shop and hotel, this building was moved from Silver City—intact—many years ago. The restaurant has been in existence for the last 12 years; it's ultra-plain, with Formica tables, but the Basque-styled dinners are terrific— a claim proven by the fact that among the clientele are many Basque immigrants.

A complete four-course meal runs about $4.00. Dinner begins with a large tureen of soup (cabbage, barley or noodle) and proceeds to side dishes of beans, corn or peas and an introductory entree of tongue, stew or spareribs. If your appetite isn't sated at this point, the meal continues with either steaks or tasty chicken dishes served with thick French fries and glasses of red house wine. Ice cream and coffee bring diners to a fulfilled silence.

There is no evidence of preheated, quick-frozen or canned foods in this home-away-from-home dining room. The basic, well-cooked food served against a noisy background is reminiscent of a visit to a large family down on the farm.

Be forewarned that J.T. Basque has a family tradition about hats. If you wear one, better hang on to it or it might just get away . . . in their traditional manner.

- *Basque*
- *760 S. Main Street, Gardnerville, Nevada*
- *Mon. - Fri. 6 - 9, Sat. & Sun 5:30 - 9*
- *Full bar*
- *No credit cards*
- *Reservations necessary for large groups*
  (702) 782-2074

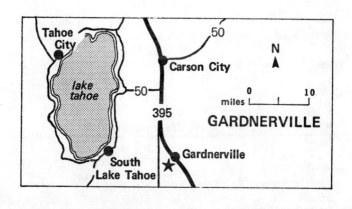

LONG VALLEY INN

We had all but abandoned our search for a hidden restaurant in the Mammoth Lakes area when a local told us about this one. We had stopped in a bar for a consoling drink, having already spent several days patrolling the area, when he joined us to mention this place "just down the road." As helpful as the man was, we hope the map is a little more helpful than the maze he drew on his beer-soaked napkin.

After a few tries, we eventually stumbled onto the Long Valley Resort just off the main highway in a very quiet country setting. It's a Chinese restaurant, and the only one in the Mammoth area that we know of.

It's a delightful hidden away spot, especially if you're looking for a feast in a scenic surrounding. Their menu is straightforward but delicious, consisting of chow mein, chop suey, noodles, egg foo yung, and several special chicken dishes. You might also want to try the steamed fish or the saute pork. As with most Chinese restaurants everything is a la carte so you can try most everything in this unusual setting in the shadows of the Sierra.

It's casual, so come as you are.

- *Basque/Chinese*
- *Lake Crowley Drive, Mammoth Lakes*
- *Daily 11 - 3 & 6 - 10*
- *Full bar*
- *No credit cards*
- *Reservations advisable (714) 935-4226*

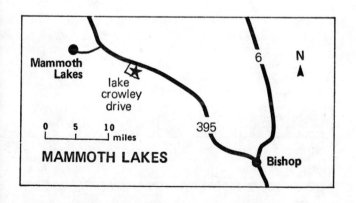

LOUIS' BASQUE CORNER

A family-run restaurant with good food in simple surroundings serving inexpensive dishes? In Reno? Louis' not only revitalized our taste buds, it also restored our earthly sanity in this one-track city. The food is outstanding.

On Mondays, featured is a lunch of cabbage or chicken-noodle soup, fresh salad with house dressing, a bowl of garbanzo beans, beef stew, chicken and rice or tripe, followed by the main course of delicious chicken and oven-baked potatoes, French bread and generous glasses of red wine. The Basques have won out again!

The evening meals are more expansive, adding to the dishes served at lunch, a bottle of wine, ice cream and coffee to top off dinner.

The entree is different every day. Tuesday the main course is pork chops and chicken-rice; Wednesday it's beef roast and tripe; Thursday, steak and beef stew; Friday, lamb roast with rice and clams; Saturday, steak and chicken-rice; Sunday, chicken and beef stew.

This restaurant is typically Basque: long family tables with bright red-and-white tablecloths brought from France, a congenial staff, lots and lots of good healthy fare and full-bodied wine.

- *Basque*
- *301 E. Fourth Street, Reno, Nevada*
- *Mon. - Fri. 11:30 - 1:30, 6 - 10; Sat. & Sun. 5 - 10*
- *Full bar*
- *BA, AE, MC*
- *Reservations for large parties only (702) 323-7203*

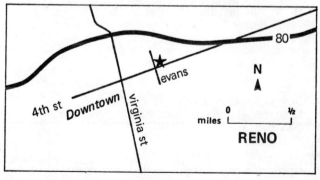

NUGGET

This is hardly what we'd call a small hidden restaurant. In fact, just because it's so big and there were too many light bulbs, we decided against a full-blown sketch. The Nugget is one of the biggest and plushest of Reno's casinos, but it does offer a choice of several separate restaurants, a few of which we felt were worth mention.

The Round House, Trader Dick's and the Circus Room were a little too high-priced for our pocket. If we'd come out winning we might have splurged, but if we had we'd have missed what we came looking for.

So we tried The Golden Rooster, tucked in a quiet corner away from the confusion and noise of gambling. Here you can count your winnings in peace or can plan out further moves to make a fast, easy buck. We arrogantly congratulated ourselves on breaking even and dug into the restaurant specials of fried chicken and Nuggets of Steak—a generous serving of tender, broiled steak chunks. Each dish included a salad, and the bill for two was under $8.00.

The Oyster Bar also offers a choice of dishes for under $3.00: oyster stew, clam chowder, gumbo fillet a la creole, shrimp pan roast, oysters on the half shell, and a combination seafood stew. The Oyster Bar opens onto the casino, however, and thus isn't as private or quiet as the Golden Rooster.

- *Steaks, plus chicken and Seafood*
- *D Street & 12th Street, Sparks, Nevada*
- *24 hours daily*
- *Full bar*
- *All major credit cards*
- *Reservations advisable (707) 358-2233*

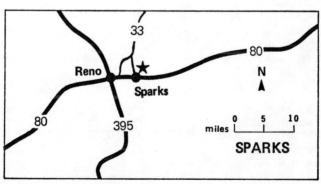

SPARKS

ST. FRANCIS HOTEL CAFE

This cheerful cafe is hidden away in the huge, non-descript St. Francis Hotel. The menu is chalked on a blackboard, which is dragged from table to table to be perused. It's a simple menu, though, with no pretentious descriptive confusion.

We started the meal with a huge serving bowl of vegetable and pasta soup; a salad of mixed greens, beets, and a variety of beans followed. We chose as our entree two pork chops so large they hardly fit on the plate—beautifully cooked, deliciously tender and succulent, with apple sauce and a baked potato with sour cream and chives. Ice cream or sherbet are offered for dessert.

The dinner steak, listed as a small top sirloin, would hardly fall under our definition of "small" and it was superbly tender. Most of the dinners are less than $4.00.

Other selections include veal cutlet, roast beef, liver and onions, chicken-fried steak, jumbo prawns, fillet of sole and lamb chops. For lunch, in addition to these dishes, a variety of sandwiches is offered at extremely reasonable prices.

City people may feel frustrated by the slow pace at the St. Francis, but all the food is prepared and cooked to order. It's really worth the extra wait, so relax and enjoy meals prepared unlike any you've had in big city restaurants.

- *American*
- *830 Main Street, Susanville*
- *Mon. - Sat. 11:30 - 2 & 6 - 10; Sun. 3 - 9*
- *Full bar*
- *BA, MC*
- *Reservations advisable (916) 257-3317*

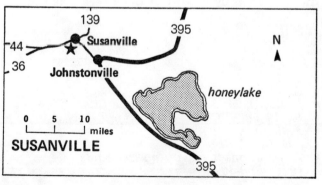

SUSANVILLE

THE HEARTHSTONE

We walked into The Hearthstone on a cold, rainy night. There really is a hearth: it's surrounded by comfy, old armchairs, and someone was just poking up the fire when we entered, tempting us to settle in for a couple of hours.

The restaurant is run by a group of young people who have bedecked this delightful scene with London street signs and all the artful trimmings of a Victorian hunting lodge. Behind the divider of books, trophies, plants and stuffed animals, our dimly lit table faced an overgrown moose head; it looked as if it had charged through the wall between two portraits of Victorian ladies, who meanwhile gazed undaunted from their gilded frames. The waiters, dressed in cheerful red overalls, fit the decor as well.

The menu here is small. There's a salad bar and, while it isn't the most prolific we've found, it does offer a change from plain lettuce. The meals under $4.00 include The Hearthstone Stew, teriyaki shrimp, and a six-ounce top sirloin. The more expensive choices include top sirloin, ribeye, teriyaki, beef kabob and spareribs.

We found a pint of draft beer and the stew, made like Mother used to make it, a good combination. Another is the small sirloin with French fries preceded by a bowl of thick vegetable soup.

- *American*
- *571 N. Lake Boulevard, Tahoe City*
- *6 - 11 daily. Closed during April, May & June*
- *Full bar*
- *AE, BA, MC*
- *Reservations necessary on weekends*
  (916) 583-4010

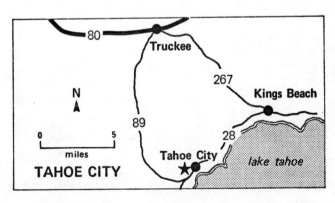

NORTHERN CALIFORNIA

Oregon

Nevada

Little River
Grass Valley
Reno

Marysville
Auburn

Sacramento

Inverness
Woodbridge
Jackson

San Rafael
Port Costa

Woodside
Hayward

Monterey
Carmel

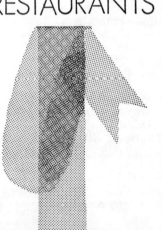

SPLURGE

RESTAURANTS

BUTTERWORTH'S

Butterworth's is so thoroughly non-commercial, it's difficult to locate. However, following directions of "just up the hill and next to the courthouse," we found the most well-preserved Victorian building in town.

Painted a crisp blue and white, the mansion sits atop a hill overlooking town and is surrounded by a precise English garden. The decor inside—also Victorian—is a picture of refined elegance.

Dinners range from $4.75 to $11.95. There's a choice of two soups, followed by salad, and the entrees include prime rib with Yorkshire pudding, chicken cordon bleu, abalone steak, marinated lamb chops, lobster or shrimp newburg, steak teriyaki, New York strip steak, and Fruit of the Bayou—lobster, scallops, shrimp and crab in a rich creamy wine sauce—the house specialty.

Lunches are offered at around $3.00. We enjoyed beef stroganoff preceded by a bowl of borscht and a fresh green salad, an interesting and surprisingly good combination. Other entrees for lunch are creole chicken over rice, oxford prime rib, and an avocado stuffed with crabmeat. In addition, there's an extensive range of salads and sandwiches such as cream cheese on nut bread, home-baked ham, and the unique crabburger.

Regardless of your usual indulgences, don't overlook the desserts. Mrs. Butterworth prepares these daily, and they're truly mouth-watering masterpieces. The key lime pie is outstanding.

- *English and Continental*
- *Lincoln Way, just south of Placer County Court House, Auburn*
- *Mon - Thurs. 11:30 - 2:30 & 5 - 9; Fri. & Sat. 11:30 - 2:30 & 5 - 10; Sun. noon - 3*
- *Beer and wine*
- *BA, MC, AE*
- *Reservations advisable, necessary on Friday & Saturday (916) 885-0249*

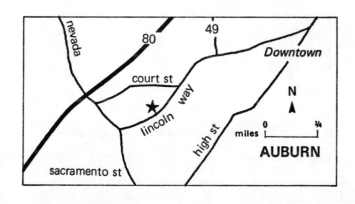

RAFFAELLO'S

In a community generously endowed with small, exclusive restaurants, Raffaello's is one of the least conspicuous. It forms part of the frontage along Misson, just below Ocean; unless you're unusually sharp you're likely to miss it, so ask a local resident for guidance.

Unlike many of Carmel's fine restaurants, Rafaello's is fairly new. It opened only eight years ago, but in that time owners Amelia and Remo d'Agliano have built up a reputation to be compared to the finest in this area.

The setting is intimate in an L-shaped dining room, but that can be a drawback: There are only about 11 tables, and reservations must be made well in advance.

Dinners include soup and salad and most are $5.50 to $6.50. The salad follows the main course, however, so try the homemade pasta, too. We sampled the Fettuccine alla Romana (fettuccine in cream with grated cheese) and the Cannelloni alla Raffaello. Both were unlike any we've had, and were great.

Among the entrees are fish, chicken and veal dishes as well as two excellent sweetbread creations. There's also Aragosta Demidoff—California lobster— for $8.00 The names of the entrees all were familiar to us, but the care and patience of Mrs. d'Agliano, the chef, added a world of understanding to our appreciation of Italian cuisine. She uses no gimmicks, takes no shortcuts; care and correctness are the essence.

- *Italian*
- *On Mission between Ocean & 7th, Carmel*
- *Mon., Wed. - Sun. 6 - 10; closed Tues.*
- *Beer and wine*
- *MC*
- *Reservations essential (408) 624-1541*

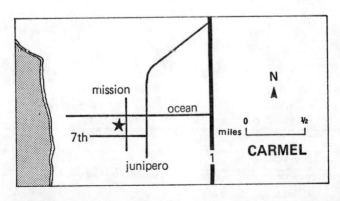

JACK'S DEER CREEK

When you think of the Mother Lode gold country, the first thoughts are usually of gold-panning, back packing, hiking, and just roughing it in general. Now, thanks to Jack's restaurant, there's a way to rough it easy and elegantly in Mother Lode country.

Elegance is their aim, and you can feel it immediately upon entering the restaurant or any of its rooms: the Garden Room, the Sacramento Room, Madam Moustache's Cabaret, or dining on the deck over-looking Deer Creek and the town. Located in a beautifully restored 115 year old building the place gives you a feeling and mood of Nevada City's colorful past as a gold rush town.

Featuring international cuisine, crisp salads, hot lunch specialties and sandwiches, Jack's has something for everyone's taste. In particular, on some special evening, try their most popular dinner: sweetbreads sauteed in white wine sauce. Other entrees may be filet of sole amandine, Oriental chicken breasts, roast leg of lamb, green pepper steak or canard aux olives. Prices range upward from $8.95 so be prepared to splurge a bit at this delightful spot. Relax and let the atmosphere take you back to the days of the Mother Lode's glorious past, even if just for an evening.

- *Continental*
- *Broad & Sacramento Sts., Nevada City*
- *Tues. - Sat. 6 - 9; Sun. 5 - 8; closed Mon.*
- *Full bar*
- *BA, MC*
- *Reservations are advised (916) 265-5809*

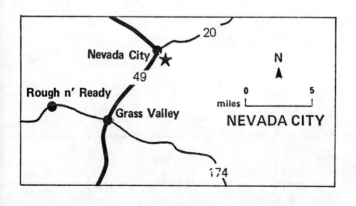

OSCAR'S BISTRO

We had heard a lot about Oscar's Bistro, but we had expected to find the Hollywood version of a French villa. Not so. In fact, the Bistro is a little white shack, slightly lopsided, that looks like it might soon be condemned. So watch carefully. It's easy to miss it as you leave the freeway and come shooting down Foothill Boulevard into Hayward.

Inside, there's a total transformation: Tiny, intimately lit rooms with small tables and wine racks as the principal decor. It's the creation of Daniel Vien-Chevreux and Don Buhrz, who have presided as host and chef for the last five years.

Dinners include a green salad, tagliarini in clam sauce and an interesting dessert. The prices range around $8.50 - $9.50 for an outstanding Poularde Braissee, tournedos or lobster thermidor. In the middle price range ($6.50 - $7.50), we recommend the frog's legs (grenouilles cannoise provencale) or the sweetbreads (ris de veau saute) served in a rich cream and mushroom sauce. The rest of the menu is predominately veal and chicken dishes, although a particular favorite is the rack of lamb for two.

The restaurant is tiny and it's popular; be sure to make reservations in advance.

- *French*
- *21181 Foothill Boulevard, Hayward*
- *Tues. - Thurs. 6 - 9:30, Fri. & Sat. 6 - 10:30; closed Sun. & Mon.*
- *Wine only*
- *AE, BA, MC*
- *Reservations essential (415) 538-3522*

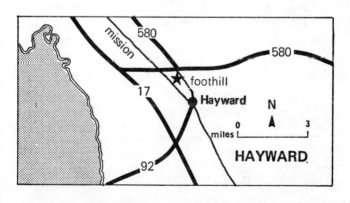

MANKA'S

Located in the Inverness Lodge on a steep hillside above Tomales Bay (you have to watch for their sign along the main road), Manka's has become one of Marin County's most renowned hidden restaurants. Owner Milan Prokupek and his wife deserve all the praise they receive for this little masterpiece.

There's an air of quiet dignity about Manka's, enhanced by crisp white tablecloths, many paintings on the walls, and an old upright piano near the entrance.

The cuisine is Eastern European (predominantly Czechoslovakian), although the generous buffet plate, which serves as the first course of a seven-course dinner, includes a number of Western European delicacies such as Norwegian herring and Danish cheese.

The selection of entrees is sensibly limited. We recommend the roast duckling with caraway sauce or the unusal beef tongue served with a delicious almond sauce; each is about $7.00. The only seafood dish is the local oysters. They are baked in the half-shell with anchovy butter, however, and they provide a refreshing change from the pan-fried oysters served in most coastal restaurants.

The desserts are served from a special cart and most are home-baked, a welcome change in this ice cream and sherbet era.

- *Czech*
- *Inverness Lodge, Inverness*
- *Mid June - Mid Sept. open 5 days; Thurs. - Mon. 6 - 8 approx.; rest of year open 3 days; Fri. - Sun. 6 - 8, except Sun. start at 4:30*
- *Beer and wine*
- *AE, MC*
- *Reservations quite necessary (415) 669-1034*

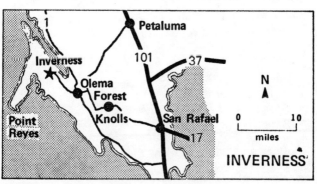

ARGONAUT INN

In 1969, Kay Sinclair came to Jackson. Equipped with a love of the Mother Lode, a self-taught cooking expertise and cartloads of antiques and tableware, she moved into the Argonaut Mine headquarters and set up her now-famous Argonaut Inn and Art Center.

Kay describes her cooking as Creative Cuisine. She uses fresh vegetables, selects her daily menu by impulse, and invents her own soups. Her efforts obviously have been a success: to meet the continual requests for her culinary secrets, she has just published a book of recipes.

A lounge of comfortable armchairs and a huge fireplace welcome guests to the Inn. The dining areas are warmly intimate, and paintings by young artists who sometimes live at the Inn are displayed on the walls.

Dinners are around $6.00 and include soup, entree, salad, coffee, or a choice of 10 to 15 different kinds of tea. A choice of three entrees is usually offered. We particularly enjoyed the Shrimp Eleanor (with mushrooms in wine-cheese sauce), the Chicken Madras (in a rich curry sauce), and the liver with wine-chutney sauce.

And for a special treat, spend an extra $1.00 for one of Kay's rich, wine soaked cakes and other unusual desserts.

- *Continental*
- *Vogan Toll Road, Jackson*
- *Tues., Wed., Fri., & Sat. 6:30 - 9; Sun. 5 - 8 (summer) or 4 - 7 (winter); closed Mon. & Thurs.*
- *Beer and wine*
- *No credit cards*
- *Reservations essential (209) 223-1475*

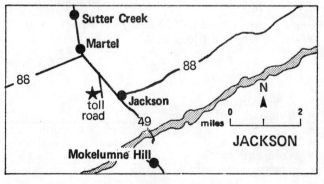

HERITAGE HOUSE

Heritage House sits tucked away off the main road on a steep wooded hillside. The original house was built in 1877, and since 1949 it's been operated by the Dennen family as a resort hotel and restaurant. Once a modest establishment, it now is a sizable complex high up on the Mendocino cliffs.

A meal at the Heritage House is like a journey through America before the days of TV dinners, frozen foods and instant everything. There's a leisurely pace here in surroundings that combine an air of domesticity and dignity. Dinners are solid American fare: baked ham, corned beef, roast turkey and pork loin, all prepared in accordance with the honored traditions of excellence.

On weeknights there is a limited choice of entrees. But on Saturday night there's a vast buffet featuring prime rib and dishes of mousaka and Oriental noodles. We were particularly impressed by the homemade soups (cream of watercress, turkey and egg strips and cream of Brussels sprouts) and the salads (hearts of romaine, avocado and citrus, molded apple and cantaloupe). If you add to this splendid fare a dessert tray of fruit and cheese, the price of around $7.00 is still in the reasonable range.

Of course, if you're a true splurger, you might wish to take advantage of the accommodation rates at the hotel, which include both breakfast and dinner for $42 to $75 a day for two persons. We wish we could join you.

- *American*
- *Route 1, Little River*
- *Daily 8 - 10 & 6:30 - 8; closed Dec. - Jan.*
- *Full bar*
- *No credit cards*
- *Reservations only (707) 937-5885*

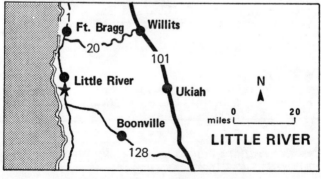

LITTLE RIVER

TONY'S

Old-timers in the area remember when this used to be a cow barn, but we have a hard time thinking of it as anything but a warm, rustic dining room. The transformation is the work of Gene and Bob Marks, who opened Tony's in 1968 as a spaghetti house and since have expanded both the barn and the menu.

Today, the range of dishes includes chicken, veal, steak and seafood—and even five variations with sweetbreads. Dinners range from $6.00 to $20.00 and up and are served with a magnificent antipasto tray, soup, salad, and a special kind of bread.

A word of warning for steak eaters: Bob will refuse to broil a steak well-done. He'll suggest that you try one of his other special entrees—chicken firenze (in a fine claret sauce) or, some of their newer entrees added since the disastrous fire of 1973 that put them out of business for nearly two years. If you're in an extravagant mood, ask Bob to prepare something special; he's a fine creative chef.

Lunches are a new feature and, while less exotic than the dinners, are a good value. The ravioli, spaghetti and French dip sandwich are in the $2.25 to $4.00 range.

Tony's is a bit hard to find, located in a semi-residential part of town surrounded by woods. Do try though since both Gene and Bob will make it more than worthwhile for your palate.

- *Continental/American*
- *1481 Hammanton Road, Marysville*
- *Tues. - Fri. 11:30 - 2 & 6 - 11; Sat. 6 - 11; Sun. 5 - 10; closed Mon.*
- *Full bar*
- *MC*
- *Reservations advisable, especially on weekends (916) 742-7102*

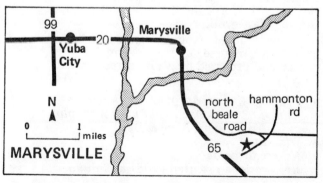

99
Marysville
20
Yuba
City
N
0   1 miles
MARYSVILLE
north
beale
road
hammonton
rd
65

MAISON BERGERAC

The menu reads "Welcome to our home," and that's how we felt inside this delightfully ornate Victorian mansion in downtown Pacific Grove. The Bergerac family moved here about four years ago, and they have created a restaurant of rare charm and quality. Betty Bergerac, assisted by her children Susanne, Janine, Lucie and Daniel, look after the diners; husband Raymond Bergerac is master chef.

The menu is unusually small, with choices of six hors d'oeuvres, eight entrees and four desserts. Dinner prices are remarkably reasonable, from $4.00 to $8.00, and include both soup and salad.

We were particularly impressed by the Basque casserole (Cassoulet Maison Bergerac), a hearty dish of lamb, sausages and white beans. If you seek the unusual, try the Tripe a la Mode de Caen (in a white wine sauce) or the fish mousse with Normandy sauce (Quennelles of Monterey Bay Sole, a true delicacy); lovers of the traditional should sample the Caneton a l'Orange (roast duckling in a rich orange and Grand Marnier sauce).

Mention must be made of the Bergerac's soups. They vary each day depending on Raymond's moods, but you can be certain—whether it's cream of carrot, cream of watercress or the outstanding St. Germain—that you will finish even the very last drop.

Desserts include Grand Marnier souffles, creme au caramel, mousse au chocolate and cheese. All superb and prepared by M. Bergerac himself.

- *French*
- *649 Lighthouse Avenue, Pacific Grove*
- *Thurs. - Sat. 6 - 9; closed Sun. - Wed. plus closed May, June, Nov. & Dec.*
- *Wine only*
- *No credit cards*
- *Reservations essential (408) 373-6996*

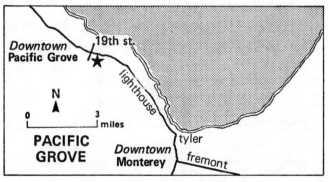

THE CLOCK

We'd heard so much praise for The Clock, we were amazed to find that it can seat only 50 patrons. Despite its size, however, we also found that its reputation is well-founded.

The decor here is fresh and lively. A huge mural set in an enclosed courtyard at the back of the restaurant dominates the dining area. It was created out of wood shingles, a fountain, and a sun-like flaming disc. There's a large garden patio, and you'll enjoy the atrium, and the fire and water sculptures.

Adding to the decor are leather and wicker chairs in the bar, framed paintings used as tables, bottle sculptures, and colored-paper murals.

There is a front courtyard, too, where lunches ranging from hamburgers to crepes are served, most for under $2.50. Diners perched on high-backed chairs find themselves lulled by the songs of near-by sparrows and the perfume of fresh flowers.

Dinners include a representative selection of international dishes in the $4.75 to $8.50 range. The homemade soups such as clam chowder (with plenty of clams) and Greek lemon soup are served with pumpernickel bread and followed by a spendidly simple salad.

Among the less expensive entrees is an excellent Poulet Bicentennial, served en casserole, and an interesting baked chicken sauterne; both under $6.00. Splurgers should try the lamb chops or the broiled filet Teriyaki marinated in a soy, ginger and pineapple sauce.

- *Continental*
- *565 Arbrego, Monterey*
- *Mon. - Fri. 11:30 - 2, 5:30 - 10; Sat. 5:30 - 10:30 Sun. 10:30 - 2 (Brunch), 5:30 - 10*
- *Full bar*
- *AE, BA, CB, DC, MC*
- *Reservations necessary for dinner only (408) 375-6100*

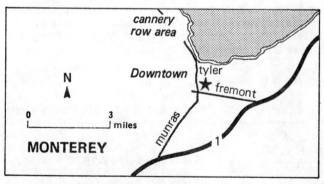

cannery
row area

Downtown

tyler

fremont

N

munras

1

0   3
|—————|—— miles

MONTEREY

BULL VALLEY INN

The Inn, located in a sturdy dressed-stone building in the unique, historical community of Port Costa, recently was taken over by Claudio Strazzabosco. News of the change alarmed some of the restaurant's devoted patrons, who considered "their" inn to be one of the finest hidden restaurants in the Bay Area.

Dear patrons, fear not! Although Claudio has made some minor changes in the menu, the quality of the Inn's cuisine remains unchanged. Each dish still is a culinary tour de force.

The French onion soup and the tossed green salad served with an unusual blue cheese vinaigrette dressing are worthy introductions. The entrees include Roast Duck Polonaise (crisp duck in a rich fruit-based sauce), two rainbow trout with shrimp filling, curried lamb chops (an unusual but tasty dish), and Chicken Romanoff with dumplings. If you really want to splurge, there is a 24-ounce Filet Mignon a la Louis XIV. Prices run from $6.00 to $12.00.

On the other hand if you would like to try this little place and watch your purse strings too, try the Armenian Dolmas for $4.95—beef stuffed grape leaves with sour cream and Greek cheese.

The decor here is authentically mid-Victorian, without the frills. There are a few interesting additions, too, such as the genuine English boar-hair dartboard near the bar. Try it for a relaxing sport after dinner or just relax in the outdoor courtyard under the black walnut trees.

- *French, Continental, American*
- *14 Canyon Lake Drive, Port Costa*
- *Thurs. 6 - 9:30; Fri. & Sat 5 10:30; Sun. 4 - 10; closed Mon., Tues. & Wed.*
- *Full bar*
- *BA, MC*
- *Reservations advisable (415) 787-2244*

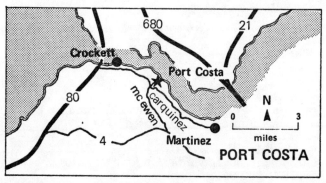

PORT COSTA

EUGENE'S

Although it's situated on one of the main highways leading to the center of Reno's loud and glittering gambling area, Eugene's is quietly relaxing and comfortably sophisticated. Here you can enjoy a little pampering, excellent service and superb food. And if you relax for a while in the secluded and very comfortable bar area, you'll find that the hustle and bustle of the outside world seems very far away.

The menu offers a splendid array of dishes from $5.00 to $10.00. The Calf Sweetbread Casserole aux Champignons is an outstanding dish; the Casserole of Beef Stroganoff is, without question, one of the best we've found; and the Filet of Beef with Bearnaise Sauce is just tremendous.

Dinners begin with your choice of French onion soup, vichyssoise, soup du jour, iced clam juice, half grapefruit or tomato juice. This is followed by a mixed green salad and the entree, served with vegetables and potatoes.

Desserts present a pleasant change: bleu cheese, port salut, fresh fruit, chocolate cream mousse, custards and sundaes. Regardless of your selection, you are assured one of the best dinners in town.

- *Continental*
- *2935 S. Virginia Street, Reno, Nevada*
- *Tues. - Sun 5 - 10:30; closed Mon.*
- *Full bar*
- *AE, BA, CB, DC, MC*
- *Reservations advisable for four or more*
  (702) 322-2089

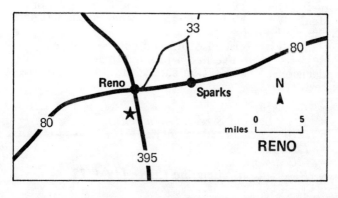

THE FIREHOUSE

It's hard to envision a clanking fire engine chugging from what now is the most elegant of restaurants. The Firehouse actually does date back to 1853, however, and it was restored by present owners Newton and Carl Cope. Now, the glistening brass pole from the original firehouse and the original brick walls mingle with magnificent Victorian decor, marble tables, fancy mirrors and old photographs in a uniquely effective display.

Three-course dinners here range from $6.00 to $14.00. But if you wish you can order a la carte and begin with such elegance as appetizers of smoked salmon, Scampi a la Maison, Escargots Bourguignonne or Avocado Garibaldi, for about $3.00.

Then come the soups, your choice of New Orleans baked onion, vichyssoise, beef consomme, consomme Madrilene, or, on Fridays only, Boston clam chowder. The soups are so delicious that a meal could be made right here.

The listing of entrees is almost as memorable to read as they are to eat. If you have at least four people and the foresight to order a day in advance, try the Suckling Imperial Boar Roast, a truly exciting experience. All other entrees are around $8.00, for delicious concoctions of noisette of lamb, Tornedos Henry IV, rack of lamb, double New York steak, Wyoming buffalo steak (when available) and chateaubriand.

The Firehouse also offers a complete menu of desserts. If you've had a problem making previous decisions, this selection surely will put you to the test.

- *American*
- *1112 Second Street, Sacramento*
- *Mon. - Fri. 11:30 - 2:30 & 6 - 10:30; closed Sun.*
- *Full bar*
- *MC*
- *Reservations advisable (916) 442-4772*

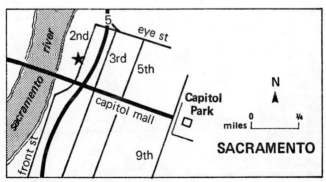

LA PETITE AUBERGE

This tiny one-story building, with its rustic brick facade, pantiled roof and delicately shuttered windows, looks out of place among the stucco monoliths of San Rafael's main street. The interior is even more unbelievable, but the checkered tablecloths and lighthearted bistro atmosphere create a perfect setting for sampling San Rafael's haute cuisine.

The menu consists almost entirely of French dishes and a selection of steaks offered both a la carte and as dinners. Dinners are in the $6.00 to $8.00 range. We were particularly impressed by the Calf's Brain Beurre Noir, the Noisette of Lamb Saute Bergere and the Quenelle of Sole. Many French restaurants are reluctant to offer quenelles because of the patience and care required to prepare them; here, however, they are excellent.

On the a la carte menu, five salads are offered, including the unusually refreshing watercress and endive for $1.35. If you decide to indulge in dessert, we suggest the outstanding Gran Marnier souffle (for two) at $4.00.

Owner Paul de Vaux, maitre d'hotel Pierre Grigaut and chef Roger Poli are to be congratulated for maintaining consistently high standards at this delightful restaurant.

- *French*
- *704 4th Street, San Rafael*
- *Tues. - Sat. 5:30 - 11, Sun. 4 - 10; closed Mon.*
- *Full bar*
- *AE, BA, MC*
- *Reservations essential (415) 456-5808*

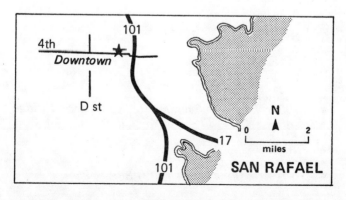

WOODBRIDGE FEED & FUEL CO.

With 107 years of history to its name, this elegant site offers a memorable dining experience. It was built as a Wells Fargo stop, later became a general store and then a tavern. Very recently it became the Woodbridge Feed & Fuel Co.

The woody interior is dominated by huge wine casks, an old-fashioned bar and charming waiters. Every evening, local talent serves as live entertainment.

There are 13 different lunch menus under $3.00, each offering five choices from the Feed List. Fresh Eggplant Parmigiano, halibut steak, rib of beef, Fettuchine Alfredo and corned beef omelette are just a sampling. There also is a New York steak sandwich for $3.95.

Dinners range from $4.25 to $7.50 and include soup, salad, garlic bread and coffee or tea. The entrees include Fillet of Sole Bonne Femme, rolled and baked with crab meat and mushrooms; Ragout of Beef with button mushrooms; Veal Francaise; and roast prime rib of beef.

- *Continental*
- *18939 N. Lower Sacramento Road, Woodbridge*
- *Mon. - Fri. 11:30 - 2 & 6 - 10, Sat. 6 - 10, Sun. 4 - 10*
- *Full bar*
- *No credit cards*
- *No reservations taken (209) 369-8295*

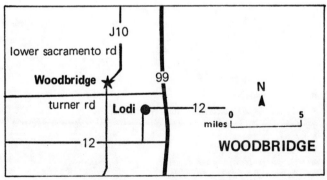

WOODBRIDGE

VILLAGE PUB

This is one of our favorite hidden splurges. The Village Pub has an atmosphere of calm and quiet conviviality. There's no ostentation, no gimmicks. The menu simply lists the dishes, without unnecessary explanations that make us wonder whether the description is a sales pitch for the dish.

The bar is delightful and is reminiscent of an English country inn. The dining rooms are paneled, and the walls are punctuated with equestrian pictures, a few of which illustrate the kingly sport of polo.

Most dinners are in the $6.00 to $9.00 range and include an excellent choice of entrees, from sweetbreads and Chicken Kiev to Veal Regina, (a rich dish served with crab's legs and asparagus in a Mornay sauce), and double lamb chops. You might also want to try their veal Antoine in a very rich cream sauce, cooked and served at your table.

Adjoining the Pub is the Pantry, a well-stocked gourmet store and delicatessen which offers the Pub's lasagne, ravioli, pizza and soups to go. Try their clam chowder, among the creamiest we've tasted.

- *Continental*
- *2967 Woodside Road, Woodside*
- *Tues. - Sat. 11:30 - 10; Sun. 4 - 10; closed Mon.*
- *Full bar*
- *AE, BA, DC, MC*
- *Reservations essential on weekends (415) 851-1294*

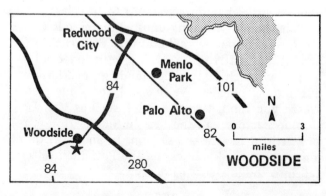

POTPOURRI

This section contains a vast range of all types of
eateries, from hamburger stands to top-class
establishments providing unusual dining-out values.
All the selections are alike in that they each offer
something a little different. We've included a lot
of places which feature outstanding breakfasts or
exceptional lunches. We've also listed some places
where you can get free samples, such as Mrs. Denson's
Cookie Factory and the Sea-Vu Smoke House, renowned for its smoked salmon. In line with the
aims of the book, almost all the Potpourri selections
fall into the low-cost category.

CHAPTER CONTENTS

Potpourri Restaurants Alphabetical By Town

NEPENTHE   Big Sur

Nepenthe is a beautiful setting high over the
Pacific and has high prices to match. But what a view!
Sandwiches vary between $2.00 and $3.50 and other
dishes range up to $6.00. The Ambrosiaburger is
excellent, the view dramatic and there's dancing outside on warm evenings.

Highway 1, 3 miles south at Big Sur State Park.
Daily 11:30 - Midnight. Full bar. AE, BA, MC.
Reservations required for parties of 6 or more

CREPES CARMEL   Carmel

One of the smallest and best snack restaurants
in Carmel! The menu consists almost entirely of
entree and dessert crepes, from 75¢ to over $4,
which contain anything from fresh honey to
creamed crab in wine. One of these huge crepes,
prepared Brittany-style and folded like an envelope
over the filling, is the perfect snack anytime.
Junipero & 6th, Carmel, in the First Federal Court.
Lunch and dinner daily. Beer and wine. No credit
cards. No reservations. (408) 624-9018.

LE BISTRO   Carmel

For one of the best hamburgers in Carmel try
the Bistro Burger at Le Bistro—a rare charbroiled
patty served on a toasted French bun with your
choice of bleu, cheddar or swiss cheese, and a tossed
salad. The price is around $2.00 but worth it. The
restaurant itself is pleasant with a place to relax on
the outside patio.
San Carlos, just south of Ocean, Carmel. Mon. - Sat.
11:30 - 9, Sun. Noon - 9 (summer), Noon - 4 (winter).
Beer and wine. No credit cards. Reservations not
required (408) 624-6545

THE TUCKBOX   Carmel

We never before stood in line for breakfast, but
here we did it willingly, despite the Carmel drizzle.
For around $2.00 we had juice, a platter of ham

and eggs, a pot of strong English tea, homemade scones and muffins and a choice of the finest marmalade and jams in California. Once you've tasted one of these hot muffins dripping with butter and olallieberry jam, breakfast will never again be quite the same. Lunches, all under $2.00, are great, too. On Tuesdays the special is beef and Yorkshire pudding.

Dolores just north of 7th Street, Carmel. Wed - Sun. 8 a.m. - 4 p.m.; closed Mon. & Tues. No bar. No credit cards. No reservations taken. (408) 624-6365.

THUNDERBIRD BOOK STORE Carmel Valley

What a great idea—combining a bookstore with an excellent snack bar serving soup-and-sandwich lunches (about $1 - $2) and buffet-style dinners (about $4)! The dining area is comfortable surrounded by shelf upon shelf of books. And the tables have chessboards built in; chess sets are loaned on request. It's a great place for an idle afternoon, and it's almost impossible to resist buying a good book to read while relaxing over your meal.

Valley Hills Center, Carmel Valley. Tues. - Sat. 10 - 10 (lunch only Sun. & Mon.). Beer and wine. BA, MC. Dinner reservations requested

RUBY'S Chico

We never found out how the heck they do it. At Chico's best greasy spoon—a favorite of the city's student population, $2.35 brings a huge, 10-ounce rib steak, four eggs, hash browns, toast, and endless refills of coffee. This is a meal that quite literally fills two plates and is a challenge to the most enthusiastic eater. Ruby's hamburgers are great, too, and the dinner specials include pork chops, lasagne and spaghetti, all for around $1.50. Amazing little place if you don't mind a bit of *greasorium Americanus.*

1st and Walnut, Chico. Mon. - Sat. 6 - 8; Sun. 8 - 2 p.m. Beer and wine. No credit cards. Reservations not necessary (916) 343-9938

ELK COVE INN   Elk

This tiny 14-guest restaurant with a "no choice" menu is the creation of Roger and Uta Noteware, a young couple from the Bay Area who set out to establish a unique guest house and restaurant on the wild Mendocino coast. Each day Uta prepares a French or German dinner, simply but superbly served with home-baked bread and fresh vegetables for around $7.00. It's a beautiful way to spend a summer evening. The view from the dining room windows, occasionally coupled with piano renditions from Roger, makes beautiful memories.

Highway 1, Elk. Daily 6:30 - 8. Beer and wine. No credit cards. Reservations essential at all times (707) 877-3321

SEAFOOD GROTTO   Eureka

Since it's owned and operated by Eureka Fisheries, you're always guaranteed fine, fresh seafood at this plain but pleasant restaurant. For lunch, try the unusual crab-burger (95¢) or the shrimp sandwich ($1.50). If the Grotto's crowded (and that happens often), go south a mile or so down Highway 101 to the Anchor. It's a fine alternative.

605 Broadway, Eureka. 11 - 10:30 daily (summer), 11 - 9:30 daily (winter). Beer and wine. AE, BA, CB, DC, MC. Reservations essential on weekends (707) 443-2075

SEA-VU SMOKEHOUSE   Eureka

Art and Lorraine Cave founded their now famous Smokehouse (not a restaurant) in an old trailer ten years ago. Although a small place, their smoked salmon and tuna are superb. Their range of canned products (seven varieties) including garlic smoked salmon and a delicious Bordelaise salmon, are all hand-packed, without preservatives. And they are generous with their samples!

4640 Broadway, Box 4964, Eureka. Daily 9:30 - 6

(Apr. 1 - Jan. 15). BA, MC. No reservations needed. (707) 442-8969.

BALCONY   Folsom

Located in this restored Gold Country town, the Balcony Cafe overlooks historic tree-shaded Sutter Street. It's a great little town for browsing on a free day, and the Balcony Cafe is a good place to stop when it's time to eat and rest. Luncheons and snacks here include soups, salads, and sandwiches plus homemade desserts.

801½ Sutter, Folsom. Tues. - Sun. 10 - 5; closed Mon. No bar. BA, MC. No reservation needed (916) 985-2605.

DICK'S CORNER   French Camp

Located in a non-descript beer bar at French Camp (5 miles south of Stockton on Highway 50), Dick's Corner serves up some of the best authentic Mexican food in the area. The a la carte dinners ($2.25 to $2.50) include chili Colorado, excellent beef enchiladas and tamales. The mole is outstanding and, if you beam at the waitress, you just might get an extra bowlful.

7400 S. Eldorado, Hwy 50, French Camp. Mon. - Sat. 11 - 11; closed Sun. Wine and beer. No credit cards. Reservations necessary on weekends (209) 982-1198

KING RICHARD'S   Grass Valley

America, watch out: The pastie is on the march and the day of the hamburger may soon be gone!

The Cornish pasties produced at King Richard's are from an old English recipe. Meat, onions, potatoes, turnips and herbs are baked inside a crisp pastry crust, folded into a half-moon. Served hot sprinkled with vinegar, they're fantastic.

King Richard's isn't a restaurant, but you can buy the pasties to go, fresh from the oven. If you want to eat them in more conducive surroundings, buy some at the Owl Tavern, right in the heart of downtown Grass Valley. Washing down Cornish pasties with a glass of strong beer is one of England's finest traditions.

251 S. Auburn Street, Grass Valley. Daily 9:30 - 6:30; closed Sun. No bar. No credit cards. No reservations taken (916) 273-0286

INVERNESS COFFEE HOUSE   Inverness

This small, rustic establishment is particularly noted locally for two dishes, its Drake's Bay Giga oysters and its unique Russian ravioli (Pelmeny). At lunchtime they're within budget range (around $2.50) and worth a special detour.

Inverness Way & Sir Francis Drake Highway, Inverness. Mon., - Fri. Noon - 3:30, 5 - 9, Sat. & Sun. 8 - 3:30, 5 - 9; closed Wed. Beer and wine. No credit cards. Reservations essential (415) 669-1109.

VLADIMIR'S   Inverness

Here's a delightful little Czechoslovakian restaurant run by Vladimir Nevl, whose colorful mini biography is printed on the back of the menu. Dinners are out of our budget range, but we suggest you try the lunches (all $3.25 and a la carte), in particular the chicken paprika or the cold duckling. A serving of Vladimir's sweet and sour cabbage is a must to complete your continental meal.

Sir Francis Drake at Inverness, Inverness. Daily noon 3 & 5 - 9; closed lunch Mon., Tue. & all day Thurs. Full bar. No credit cards. (415) 669-1021

AL'S PLACE   Locke

A generous New York steak served with—would you believe?—toasted French bread and gobs of peanut butter and marmalade is the specialty here. Sounds yukky, but it's absolutely fantastic. Lunches are priced at a low $1.75. Dinners unfortunately were a little above our price range.

Al's has the simplest of dining rooms—very

informal and relaxing, in the floppy sense! The
adjoining bar resembles a junk room featuring
dollars tacked on the ceiling, business cards
pinned to the walls, old animal heads, and a huge
stuffed ostrich. A terrific place, right in the heart
of the fascinating Chinese delta community of Locke.

Locke. Mon. - Sat. 11:30 - 2 & 5 - 10, Sun. 3 - 10.
Full bar. No credit cards. No reservations necessary
(916) 777-1800

LITTLE RIVER CAFE   Little River

This is one of the smallest, least conspicuous
restaurants we have yet found. But the International Dinners served on weekends ($3.25 to
$3.75) are truly exceptional, and owner/cook
Kirk Petersen is to be praised. If you're lucky,
you may find he's serving his favorite Mozambique
dish—Peixe a Lumbo, a delicious stew of red
snapper and shrimps. Keep cooking, Kirk!

76 Station, Little River. Daily 9 - 4 & 5 - 9:30.
Beer and wine. No credit cards. No reservations taken

LA HACIENDA INN   Los Gatos

A local tradition in the Los Gatos/Saratoga
area is La Hacienda's Sunday brunch. Prices
range from $1.95 to $4.75 for a choice of omelettes,
eggs Benedict, prime rib sandwich or poached eggs a
la Reine. A very pleasant way to start a mellow Sunday, especially in a building formerly a stage stop.
and a governor's hunting lodge more than 200
years ago.

Hwy. 9 midway between Saratoga & Los Gatos. Mon -
Sat. 11 - 11; Sun. 11 - 10. Full bar, AE, BA, CB,
DC, MC. Reservations advisable. (408) 345-9230

VILLAGE HOUSE   Los Gatos

This delightful luncheon restaurant under a sprawl-
ing oak tree always seems to be full of Los Gatos ma-
trons enjoying fine food at reasonable prices. Select
from delectables such as quiche Lorraine, salmon pie,

dolmas or chicken crepes including salad, at only
$3.25 . All profits here go to charity, and the
cooks are all talented volunteers.

*Village Square, Los Gatos. Mon. - Fri. Noon - 1:15;
closed Sat. & Sun. Beer and wine. No credit cards.
Reservations essential (408) 354-1040*

THE STOVE   Mammoth Lakes

Elegant and extravagant restaurants abound in
Mammoth Lakes, but there's a noticeable shortage
of good, inexpensive places to grab a quick snack
before beating the multitudes to the ski slopes.

The Stove, located on old Mammoth Road, is an
exception and is deservedly popular for its huge
breakfasts, sandwiches and outstanding daily
specials. Here you can feast on such dishes as
liver and onions, corned beef and cabbage, chow
mein, pork chops or fried chicken for around $1.85.

Try the homemade soups, too. We had an outstanding cream of spinach for 45¢.

*Old Mammoth Road. Daily 6 a.m. - 4 p.m.
No bar. No credit cards. No reservations needed.
(714) 934-2821.*

ALLIED ARTS GUILD   Menlo Park

Situated on the northern fringe of the Stanford
University campus (west on Cambridge Avenue
from El Camino Real) is the Allied Arts Guild, a
fascinating complex of craft and dress shops
modeled after a similar complex in Barcelona. It
was built during the 1930s on a portion of the
vast Rancho de las Pulgas.

Lunch at the Guild Tea Room is gourmet fare,
and the three-course meal ($3.50) usually includes
an excellent casserole entree prepared by volunteers.
All profits go to the Children's Hospital at Stanford.

For an alternative, try the Stanford Barn, also
on the northern fringe of the campus. This international cafeteria, with its outdoor patio, is a
popular lunch spot.

Arbor Road and Creek Drive, Menlo Park.

Mon. - Sat. Noon - 2:30, Mon. - Fri. tea, 3 - 5;
closed Sun. No bar. No credit cards. Reservations
essential. (415) 324-2588.

OASIS   Menlo Park

For some of the best hamburgers on the Peninsula, try this old beer hall with its rough-topped
tables and pin-ball machines. Note the great
selection of beers including England's Watneys,
Australia's Swan, and China's Tsingtao in addition
to draft steam beer. A raucous, fun place.

241 El Camino Real, Menlo Park. Daily 11 a.m. -
2 a.m. Beer only. No credit cards. Reservations
not necessary (415) 326-8896.

FLORA'S   Monterey

Ever had the urge to build yourself a six-inch-
thick sandwich bulging with ham, salami, chicken,
pork, turkey, beef, bologna, jack cheese, Swiss
cheese, pate and relishes galore? At Flora's, on
Cannery Row, it's an everyday lunchtime occurrence—
for a meager 50¢.

Next door is Capone's, a barn-like place which
can be reached through Flora's Victoriana bar. At
Capone's, pizzas are served with beer along with
spaghetti/ravioli concoctions in gallon-sized portions.
A great combination.

Capone's Warehouse, Cannery Row, Prescott.
Daily 11 a.m. - 2 a.m. Full bar. No credit cards.
No reservations needed.

LOVER'S POINT INN   Monterey

The name of this restaurant just about tells it all—
about the dramatic view overlooking the Pacific
coastline and the crashing surf. It's a place to come
to see and to stroll about even if you're not hungry,
but if you are, Lover's Point Inn is there for breakfast, lunch, or dinner. About as good a bargain as can
be found anywhere is the champagne steak dinner for
two at $10.95, which includes all the trimmings.
Daily specials, around $3.00 to $4.00, include Irish
stew and beef stroganoff to help stretch the budget,

while enjoying the free view.
*Foot of Ocean View Blvd., Pacific Grove. Daily
8 a.m. - 10 p.m. Full bar. Major credit cards. Reservations advised. (408) 372-7787.*

THE FLYING LADY   Morgan Hill

Although newly established, the Flying Lady has
developed a solid reputation in the San Jose area
for its buffet lunches. For less than $3.00, the 20-
dish selection may include shrimp curry, lasagne,
turkey, and beef stew. The restaurant, which is
part of the impressive Hill Country project, has a
distinct aeronautical flavor and a spendid view
over the Morgan Hill valley. An inspiring place
for lunch!

*15060 Foothill Avenue, Morgan Hill. Wed. - Sun.
11 - 2 & 6 - 9:30. Full bar. BA, MC. Reservations
essential on weekends (408) 227-4607 — 779-4136.*

NATIONAL HOTEL   Nevada City

As soon as you enter the Victorial barroom of
the National Hotel you're back in the boom days of
the Gold Rush, when opulence verged on the extreme
and buildings dripped with gingerbread and exotic
wrought-iron trimmings.

Here, for about $2.50 you can feast on a hot plate
special, sandwiches, or their special Gold Country
luncheons. Thrown in free is a trip to yesteryear.

*211 Broad Street, Nevada City. Daily Noon - 2:30.
Full bar. BA, MC. Reservations not required (916)
265-4851*

THE WHARF   Noyo (Ft. Bragg)

Unfortunately, the dinners at this delightful
seafront restaurant are just a little too expensive
for inclusion in our budget section. But the
lunches are great and they're reasonable. In
particular, try the ling cod, the salmon, or the
Friday crab omelette, all for around $2.25.
*780 N. Harbor Drive, Noyo (near Fort Bragg).
Mon. - Sun. 11 - 10. Full bar. No credit cards.*

Reservations necessary during summer
(707) 964-4283.

LONDON HOUSE   Palo Alto

Imagine eating English delights—delicately
poached salmon and cucumber sandwiches, crumpets or flaky sausage rolls, with real (alcoholic)
Devonshire cider or English tea served from a huge
teapot—in Palo Alto! The London House is a
charming peek into merry old England. At around
$3.00 for lunch and their specials, it's an unbeatable
experience. An incredible price!
630 Ramona Street. 1/2 block south of Hamilton,
Palo Alto. Tues. - Sat. 11 - 11; closed Sun. & Mon.
Full bar. BA, MC. No reservations necessary
(415) 321-0773.

SHAIKH'S   Palo Alto

At last, an Indian restaurant with super-low
prices! Admittedly, it's just about as plain as you
could get; you get your own food at the counter,
and it's served on plastic plates. But the curries
($1.65 to $1.85) prepared by Mrs. Shaikh are
superbly pungent, and her side dishes of samosas,
pakodas and chapatis are as good as those served
at San Francisco's more expensive Indian restaurants.
393 California, Palo Alto. Mon. - Sat. 11 - 8:30;
closed Sun. No bar. No credit cards. No reservations
needed (415) 327-6555.

VESUVIO   Placerville

If you get a yearning for good seafood or Italian
way up in the Mother Lode, try Vesuvio's in Placerville. For some fifteen years now they have offered
specials such as gourmet prawns, homemade pizza,
lasagne, giant scallops, lobster tails, and Dungeness
crab, all in the $3.00 to $4.00 range.

251 Main Street, Placerville, Wed., Thurs. 11 - 2 &
5 - 10; Fri. & Sat. 11 - 2 & 5 - 2 a.m., Sun. 5 - 10;
closed Mon. Beer and wine. No credit cards.

Reservations helpful for lunch and on weekends.
(916) 622-9975

CRYSTAL TAVERN   Red Bluff
   Although the Crystal Tavern's dinner prices
tend to be a little high, their Chef's Table is one
of the best bargains in the valley. $2.75 gives you
a free rein at the extensive salad bar plus your
choice of a chicken, roast beef or baked ham
entree. An excellent value.
343 S. Main Street, Red Bluff. Mon. - Sat. 5 - 11,
Sun. 2 - 10. Full bar. BA, MC. Reservations not
necessary on weekends (916) 527-0880

THE SWEET SHOPPE   Red Bluff
   The Sweet Shoppe offers an international
selection of candies and sundaes as well as sandwiches and daily specials. Featured here are sandwiches of corned beef, pastrami, turkey, egg salad or
ham, all under $2.00 and truly delicious. And even
more importantly they specialize in 5-scoop banana
splits, real soda and floats, and lemonades and lime-
ades in the rough. This is a charming tearoom with
homemade toys from all over the world, crockery,
glassware and delicious candies.
   If you're solo, sit at the Introduce Yourself table
and meet all who enter.
402 Pine Street, Red Bluff. Mon - Thurs. & Sat.
9 - 6, Fri. 9 - 5, except 9 - 10 p.m. June - Sept.;
closed Sun. No bar. MC. Reservations not
necessary (916) 527-0487

MRS. DENSON'S   Redwood Valley
   This isn't a restaurant, it's a cookie factory—
where you'll be handed cookie samples with a
superb cup of Kona coffee as soon as you walk
in the door. They make every conceivable kind
of cookie here (including dark, rich jumbo oat-
meal cookies—our favorite) in addition to fruit

cakes and cereal-based health foods. It's a great little place to pause for a few minutes as you zip along the Redwood Highway.

9651 Highway 101, Redwood Valley. Mon. - Fri. 8 - 6, Sat. & Sun. 9 - 5. No bar. BA, MC. (707) 485-7307.

SQUEEZE INN   Reno

The way the casino complex is expanding downtown Reno, the tiny Squeeze Inn may well find itself squeezed out in a short time. Meanwhile, this cramped little diner, with its Formica tables, juke box and omnipresent slot machines, serves superb sandwiches and soul-food dishes including snow white chitterlings, navy beans and ham, smothered chicken and rice, lean lamb stew, and a chili that would be hard to match anywhere. Most dinners are well under $3.00 and include homemade soup and fresh, hot corn muffins. For an extra 5¢ try a side of giblet dressing.

344 N. Virginia Street, Reno. 24 hours daily. No bar. No credit cards. No reservations taken (702) 786-9911

MANZANITA ROOM   Rescue

Set along a narrow country road near the small town of Rescue is this great smorgasbord restaurant. The owners, Chips and Betty Franklin, only open the place on weekends, but they serve huge, eat-all-you-can meals for $3.00 a head. The Franklins offer a staggering array of dishes including beef, ribs, ham, turkey, chicken, pork, stuffed peppers, and Swiss steak as well as soup, salad, homemade cobblers for dessert and coffee. It's hard to resist any of it.

2 miles west of Rescue on the road to Folsom. Fri. & Sat. 5 - 10, Sun. noon - 8. No bar. No credit cards. No reservations taken.

LI'L JOES   Sacramento

Stuck in a brand-new shopping center in the northeast sector of Sacramento, Li'l Joe's normally wouldn't warrant a second glance. But try the broil-it-yourself steaks—huge T-bones and New Yorks, all well-aged—at the ridiculously low price of $1.00 (yes, $1.00). Side dishes are a few cents extra, not that they're needed. A fun place for an ultra-low-cost dinner.

1250 Howe Avenue, Sacramento. Open 24 hours every day. No bar. No credit cards. Reservations not taken (916) 925-8731

MANSSUR'S SHISH KABOB   San Jose

It was like walking into a Tehran bazaar—the smell of barbecued kabobs, a huge silver samovar and mounds of long-grain Iranian rice. Manssur's is a very small informal place open for lunch and dinner. Try the kabob or the kabob kubideh sandwiches—fantastic at 99¢ and $1.25. If you're looking for real authenticity, there's chelo kabob and khoresht. Only one flaw: Manssur uses beef rather than lamb. He claims American lamb is too fatty.

3rd and San Salvador, San Jose. Mon. - Sat. 4 - 10 p.m., closed Sun. Beer and wine. No credit cards. No reservations needed (408) 295-7223.

MARIPOSA HOUSE   San Juan Bautista

Norma, Becky, and Wanda chose this beautiful little mission town to turn a tiny 1920s house into a gourmet's delight. Serving luncheon only—except for Monday's boarding house night—they offer a varying choice of international cooking which includes Jambon en Casserole, Salad San Juan, almost no calorie Ceviche, and in August— freshly picked corn-on-the-cob.

We tried the fresh corn cooked 4 minutes to perfection, the Ceviche, along with some of their fine sherry. It was all good and along with the small town atmosphere gave us a pleasant feeling about how times must have been when the pace of life was a bit slower and perhaps more enjoyable.

4th and Mariposa Sts. San Juan Bautista. Luncheon 11:30 - 3 daily, closed Thurs.; Dinner 6 - 9 Mon. only. Wine list. No credit cards. (408) 623-4666

EAST OF EDEN   Salinas

This old wooden turn-of-the-century church in
the middle part of town has been rededicated to
serve the gourmet's palate. The pews have been
removed to make room for the tables, ferns and
other greenery, but the beautiful altar remains.
In an area where it's difficult to find a good place
to eat, this is a heavenly place to enjoy excellent
steaks and seafoods in the $5.00 price range.

*327 Pajaro St., Salinas. Lunch Mon. - Fri. 11:30 -
2., dinner Sun. - Thurs. 5:30 - 10 & Fri. & Sat.
5:30 - 11. BA, MC. Wine. (408) 424-0819.*

COOPER HOUSE   Santa Cruz

If you'd like to savor a fresh mushroom casserole
while sitting outside underneath a Cinzano umbrella
as people pass by, this is your place! On beautiful
tree-lined Cooper Street, this restaurant in the old
courthouse building offers a wide variety of foods—
sandwiches, salads, fabulous breads plus there's a
good wine list. And it is right next door to the Octa-
gon, Santa Cruz's unique historical museum. Your
$3.00 lunch here will be a unique experience in
leisurely people watching if you come in the summer.

*110 Cooper St. Downtown Santa Cruz. Luncheon
11:30 - 3, dinner 3 - 10 daily. Beer and wine. No
credit cards. Reservations not necessary.
(408) 423-4444.*

MARSHALL HOUSE   Santa Rosa

Marshall House is one of the daintiest tea rooms
we have yet found. Located a few blocks south of
downtown Santa Rosa in an old residential area,
this white Victorian mansion is an interior decorator's
delight, thanks to the skill and taste of owner
Harriet Watson. Only lunches are served in the
charming dining rooms, but it's very much a
favorite of the ladies of Santa Rosa. The entrees
are limited but include casseroles and souffles

served with an eye-catching array of desserts. Be sure
to visit the interesting craft shops in the upstairs
rooms. Luncheons are about $3.00.
*835 Second Street. Mon. - Sat. 11 - 2:30 p.m.;
closed Sun. No bar. No credit cards. Reservations advisable. (707) 542.5305.*

LA MERE MICHELLE Saratoga

This dainty little restaurant offers some of the
best luncheon values on this part of the Peninsula.
We particularly recommend the boeuf bourguignon,
the veal scallopine, or the filet of sole amandine, all
$2.50 to $3.75. Dinner specialties include an excellent
veal piccata maison, filet of beef Andreeff (sauteed
slices of filet, with shallots, mushrooms, red wine,
demi-glace), and their extra special fresh poached sal-
mon-hollandaise. Prices range from $5.75 to $8.25
for dinner served with unhurried service.
*14482 Big Basin Way, Saratoga. Tues. - Fri.
11:30 - 2 & 6 - 9:30, closed Sun. & Mon. Beer
and Wine. BA, MC. Reservations (408) 867-5272*

JUANITA'S Glen Ellen

This is one of the most exotic restaurants we
have visited, and in the gastronomic wilderness of
the wine valleys it's a culinary oasis. The buffet
dinner offers about 22 dishes, five of which are
meat-based, for $3.50. But the real bonanza is
the 32-ounce prime rib (serves at least two) for
about $8.00. Now located at the Old Water Wheel
in Jack London Village after the last place in Sonoma
burned down—Juanita has brought all her traditions
and charm along. Ole!
*Arnold Dr. about one-half mile south of town, Glen
Ellen. Daily 9 a.m. - 11. Full bar. BA, MC.
Reservations necessary on weekends (707) 996-7010*

THE COURTYARD Soquel

The once-exclusive Courtyard recently changed
hands, and menu/price changes have made the
restaurant more accessible to the budget-con-

204 / HIDDEN RESTAURANTS

scious diner. Although dinners still are a little
beyond our range, Bill Skwarek's Beggar's Banquet lunch is a bargain at $2.00—tossed salad,
soup, homemade bread and cheeses. There are
many other original dishes, too. The $6.00 Sunday
brunch, with free-flowing champagne, is a delightful
"splurge" experience.

*2591 Main Street, Soquel. Tues. - Sat. 11:30 - 2:30,
6 - 10, Sun. 6 - 10; closed Mon. Beer and wine.
AE, BA, MC. Reservations advisable (408) 476-2529*

HARVEY'S RESORT HOTEL   So. Lake Tahoe

Gourmands, here is your nirvana! In the plush
opulence of this Nevada establishment, a bacchanal
banquet that would have put Henry VIII's efforts
to shame awaits you. If you're a fish lover, try
the Friday-night buffet with lobster, trout, and
prawns. Meat-eaters, there's a Saturday buffet
featuring prime rib and top sirloin. All for around
$4.00. Amazing value!

*Highway 50, Stateline, Nevada. Mon. - Sat. 5 - 11,
Sun. 4 - 10. Full bar. All major cards. Reservations
essential (702) 588-2411*

LOS AGUIRRE'S   So. Lake Tahoe

This crowded, cluttered little place with its
strange Swiss facade always seems full of young
and noisy but hungry people. The menu and prices
are standard for a low-cost Mexican restaurant,
but the food is outstanding and the dishes are
prepared individually. We suggest the chili rellenos
smothered in a rich cheese sauce, the beef enchiladas
and the tamales. More expensive but excellent for
the cost is the Steak Picado, top sirloin chunks in a
rich sauce, served with salad, refried beans and rice.

*2212 Highway 50, S. Lake Tahoe. Mon. - Fri. 4 - 10:3
Sat. 4 - 11, Sun. 4 - 10. Beer only. No credit cards. N
reservations taken (916) 541-9849*

POOR PIERRE'S   So. Lake Tahoe

If you're caught between the extravagant-plush and mediocre-cheap restaurants of South Lake Tahoe, try Poor Pierre's. Set back from the road behind tall trees, it offers an excellent variety of snacks and sandwiches served cafeteria-style. Most items are under $1.00. Try the French dip sandwich thick with sliced roast beef, the homemade chili or the barbecued beef sandwich, all served with your choice of salad and relishes. For the more extravagant, there's a 10-ounce New York steak dinner for $4.25, served in the adjoining intimately-lit bar.

Highway 50, South Lake Tahoe. Mon. - Sat. 11 - 8; closed Sun. Full bar. No credit cards. No reservations taken (916) 544-4237

YUT WAH   Stockton

Three tables and a small counter are all there is to this totally informal but spotless restaurant. The clientele is almost entirely Chinese, which always gives a good indication of the authenticity of the food. The simply prepared dishes, all less than $2.00, include such unusual fare as salty fish on steamed pork, fried prawns with shells, bitter melon chicken, curry spareribs and Chinese string beans with beef. Lunches are even less, around $1.50, and they're among the best and tastiest bargains we found in Stockton.

133 E. Washington, Stockton. Daily 10:30 - 7. No bar. No credit cards. No reservations taken.

SUTTER CREEK BEER GARDEN   Sutter Creek

Again we return to the days of wooden floors that creak, honky-tonk pianos, sepia portraits, gilded mirrors and spacious restrooms! Although the Beer Gardens is known for its Mexican food, we enjoyed an outstanding oversized top sirloin dinner steak with French fries for $4.15. After a mellow dinner

here you can almost see the gold miners of old
standing 'round the bar telling their stories.
*76 Main Street, Sutter Creek. Mon., Tues., Thurs. &
Fri. 11 - 2, 4:30 · 9, Sat. & Sun. 11 - 9; closed Wed.
Wine, beer, and champale. No credit cards.
No reservations taken (209) 267-9852*

VILLAGE INN   Shingle Springs

The Shingle Hilton—as it's known locally—is housed
in a building dating to the gold days of the 1800s,
when this tiny town was even larger than Placerville.
Food specialties here include a delectable Brandy fried
chicken, which we enjoyed, as well as an offering of
steaks and seafoods in the $6.00 to $7.00 range. An
old country store is next door.
*Mother Lode Dr. Downtown Shingle Springs.
Daily 9 a.m. - 11 p.m. Full bar. BA, MC.
Reservations advisable on weekends (916) 677-2259.*

PIETRO'S   Vacaville

If you like thick-crust pizza laden with pepperoni,
mushrooms, sausage, peppers and onions on a rich
cheese and tomato base, this is your place. It's
just off Main Street; for a pizzeria, it's remarkably
plush. The 16-inch-diameter large-size pizzas can
cost up to $5.00, but they provide a full meal for
two or three people.
*407 Cernon Street, Vacaville. Daily 11 a.m. - Mid-
night. Beer and wine. BA. Reservations necessary
on weekends (707) 446-1771*

GIUSTI'S   Walnut Grove

Here you can enjoy lunch of a bottle of wine
and your choice of at least two specials from the
list of pork chops, tripe, spareribs, top sirloin,
hamburger steak, fillet of sole or ham hocks and
lima beans, plus salad and soup. And all for less
than $2.50. For dinner, the entrees of seafood,
steaks, chicken, veal and pasta are served with
soup, salad and a relish tray. The bar tends to fill

up with locals watching whatever sports are on
television, but the separate dining area is quiet
and private.

*Old Levee Road, Walnut Grove. Tues. - Fri. Noon -
1:30 & 5 - 10; closed Sat. - Mon. Full bar. No
credit cards. No reservations taken (916) 776-1808*

COBWEB PALACE   Westport

Richly adorned in true 1890s style, the Palace
is a great little place to stop for homemade soup,
bread, burgers and chili on your way along the
shoreline highway. Dinners in the $2.25 to $3.95
range are simple but prepared with care. On weekends, the dance floor is opened up and this be-
comes a wild and lively place.

*Main Street, Westport. Daily 7 - 10, 11 - 2 & 6 - 9.
Full bar. No credit cards. Reservations necessary on
weekends (707) 964-2994*

CHUTNEY KITCHEN   Yountville

Vintage 1870, located in an old winery just off
Route 29 in Yountville, is another one of those
shopping and browsing complexes like The Cannery
in San Francisco. It's extremely well-designed,
and it provides a welcome diversion from the
ceaseless elbow-bending on a wine-tasting tour of
the Napa Valley. The Chutney Kitchen, located
in the heart of the complex, offers a small but
excellent variety of salads and sandwiches ($.75 to
$2.75) in addition to homemade soups and a daily
luncheon special. (The chicken curry mousse is exceptional.) Also visit the adjoining Chutney counter
for free tasting.

*Vintage 1870. Tues. - Sun. Noon - 5; closed
Mon. No bar. No credit cards. No reservations
taken. (707) 944-2788.*

NORTHERN CALIFORNIA

Oregon

REGIONS

THE HIGH COUNTRY

Nevada

THE
CENTRAL
VALLEY

THE COAST

THE GOLD COUNTRY

SAN FRANCISCO
FRINGE

INDEXES

RESTAURANTS BY REGION

SAN FRANCISCO FRINGE

City	Restaurant	Cuisine	Page
Port Costa	Bull Valley Inn	French	174
Port Costa	Warehouse Cafe	American/Basque	36
San Jose	Manssur's	Iranian	201
San Jose	Original Joe's	Italian/American	38
San Mateo	Pot Sticker	Chinese	42
San Rafael	La Petite Auberge	French	180
Santa Rosa	Marshall House	American	202
Saratoga	La Mere Michelle	French	203
Sebastopol	Le Pommier	French	44
Sonoma	Juanita's	American	203
Sonoma	La Casa	Mexican	46
Soquel	Courtyard	American	203
Vacaville	Pietro's	American/Italian	206
Woodside	Village Pub	Continental	184
Yountville	Chutney Kitchen	American	207

COAST

City	Restaurant	Cuisine	Page
Big Sur	Big Sur Inn	American	50
Big Sur	Nepenthe	American	189
Carmel	Clam Box	Seafood	52
Carmel	Crepes Carmel	Crepes	189
Carmel	French Poodle	French	54
Carmel	Le Bistro	Steaks/Sandwiches	189
Carmel	Raffaello	Italian	156
Carmel	Thunderbird Book Store	Sandwiches/Buffet Dinners	190
Carmel	Tuck Box	Breakfasts	189
Crescent City	Harbor Grotto	Seafood	58
Elk	Elk Cove Inn	Continental	191

City	Restaurant	Cuisine	Page
Eureka	Lazio's	Seafood	60
Eureka	Seafood Grotto	Seafood	191
Eureka	Sea-Vu Smoke House	Smoked Fish	191
Fort Bragg	Piedmont Hotel	Seafood/American/Italian	64
Fort Bragg	Wharf	Seafood	197
Garberville	Benbow Inn	Continental	66
Little River	Heritage House	American	166
Little River	Little River Cafe	International	194
Mendocino	Sea Gull	Seafood	68
Monterey	Clock	Continental	172
Monterey	Consuelo's	Mexican	70
Monterey	Flora's	Drinks/Pizza/Sandwiches	196
Monterey	Fuki Sushi	Japanese	72
Monterey	Maison Bergerac	French	170
Monterey	Lover's Point	American	196
Redwood Valley	Mrs. Denson's	Snacks	199
Salinas	East of Eden	Steaks	202
Samoa	Samoa Cookhouse	American	62
San Juan Bautista	La Casa Rosa	American	56
San Juan Bautista	Mariposa	Continental	201
Santa Cruz	Cooper House	American	202
Santa Cruz	Santa Cruz Hotel	Italian	74
Westport	Cobweb Palace	American	207

CENTRAL VALLEY

City	Restaurant	Cusine	Page
Chico	Italian Cottage	Italian	78
Chico	Ruby's	American	190
Corning	J & W Cafe	American	80
French Camp	Dick's Corner	Mexican	192
Locke	Al's Place	Steaks	193
Los Molinos	N - B Restaurant	American	82

City	Restaurant	Cuisine	Page
Marysville	Tony's	Continental/American	168
Modesto	Carmen's	Mexican	84
Paradise	Pinocchio's	Seafood	86
Red Bluff	Crystal Tavern	American	199
Red Bluff	Sweet Shoppe	Snacks	199
Redding	Jack's Grill	American	88
Redding	Ramona's	Mexican	90
Sacramento	Firehouse	American	178
Sacramento	Fuji's Sukiyaki	Japanese	92
Sacramento	Hong Kong Cafe	Chinese	94
Sacramento	Li'l Joe's	Steaks	200
Sacramento	Sam's Rancho Villa	American	96
Sacramento	Woodbridge Feed	Continental	182
Stockton	On Lock Sam	Chinese	98
Stockton	Ospital's Basque	Basque	100
Stockton	Ye Olde Hoosier	American	102
Stockton	Yut Wah	Chinese	205
Walnut Grove	Giusti's	American	206
Yuba City	Lee's Canton	Chinese/American	104

THE GOLD COUNTRY

City	Restaurant	Cuisine	Page
Auburn	Auburn Hotel	Basque	108
Auburn	Butterworth's	Continental/English	154
Auburn	Cafe Delicias	Mexican	110
Buena Vista	Paul's Boarding House	American	112
Cedar Ridge	Dragon Seed Inn	Chinese	114
El Dorado	Poor Red's	American	116
Folsom	Balcony	Snacks	192
Folsom	Joe & Dodies	American	118
Folsom	Manzanita Room	Smorgy	200
Georgetown	Buckeye Lodge	American	120
Grass Valley	King Richard's	English	192
Grass Valley	Schiedel's	German	124

City	Restaurant	Cuisine	Page
Jackson	Argonaut Inn	Continental	164
Jackson	Wheel Inn	Italian	128
Nevada City	1890 House	Continental	122
Nevada City	Jack's Deer Creek	Continental	158
Nevada City	National Hotel	Smorgy	197
Placerville	Vesuvio	Italian/Seafood	198
Sutter Creek	Sutter Creek Beer Gardens	Mexican/American	205
Wallace	Rossetti's	American/Italian	126

HIGH COUNTRY

City	Restaurant	Cuisine	Page
Alturas	Rancho Steak House	American	132
Bishop	Long Valley Resort	Basque	142
Cedarville	Golden's	American	134
Chester	Mt. Lassen Club	Steaks	136
Chester	Timber House	American	138
Gardnerville	J.T. Basque	Basque	140
Mammoth Lakes	Stove	American	195
Nevada	Harvey's Resort	American	204
Reno	Eugene's	Continental	176
Reno	Louis' Basque Corner	Basque	144
Reno	Nugget	Chicken/Seafood/Steak	146
Reno	Squeeze Inn	Soul food	200
S. Lake Tahoe	Los Aguirre's	Mexican	204
S. Lake Tahoe	Poor Pierre's	American	205
Shingle Springs	Village Inn	American	206
Susanville	St. Francis Cafe	American	148
Tahoe City	Hearthstone	American	150

RESTAURANTS BY CUISINE

AMERICAN

Big Sur Inn	50
Buckeye Lodge	120
Chutney Kitchen	207
Cobweb Palace	207
Cooper House	202
Courtyard	203
Cranberry House	20
Crystal Tavern	199
Elegant Bib	40
Firehouse	178
Flying Lady	197
Giusti's	206
Golden's	134
Harvey's Resort	204
Hearthstone	150
Heritage House	166
Inverness Coffee House	193
Jack's Grill	88
J & W Cafe	80
Jerry's Farmhouse	30
Joe & Dodies	118
Juanita's	203
La Casa Rosa	56
Lover's Point	196
Marshall House	202
N - B Restaurant	82
Nepenthe	189
Oasis	196
Paul's Boarding House	112
Pietro's	206
Poor Red's	116
Poor Pierre's	205
Rancho Steak House	132
Ruby's	190
Samoa Cookhouse	62
Sam's Rancho	96
St. Francis Cafe	148
Stove Restaurant	195
Timber House Lodge	138
Village Inn	206
Warehouse Cafe	36
Ye Olde Hoosier Inn	103

BASQUE

Auburn Hotel	108
J.T. Basque	140
Long Valley Resort	142
Louis' Basque	144
Ospital's Basque	100

BRITISH

London House	198
Tuck Box	189

CHINESE

Dragon Seed Inn	114
Hong Kong Cafe	94
Lee's Canton	104
On Lock Sam	98
Pot Sticker	42
Yut Wah	205

CONTINENTAL

Argonaut Inn	164
Allied Arts Guild	195
Benbow Inn	66
Clock	172
Elk Cove Inn	191
Eugene's	176
1890 House	122
Jack's Deer Creek	158

RESTAURANTS BY NAME

A Special Notice to our readers:

Excellence is our publishing aim—to provide the best, most accurate and timely information in the world about travel/ adventure, good food and wine, all at the very lowest prices. We have discovered that you don't have to spend a fortune to enjoy dining out or travel. You just have to know where to go.

To speed making our latest information available to the adventurous, we have just started the Newwest California Club which will present monthly, the very latest of the very best. . .and all for not much money. Try it and see.

Newwest California Club Membership

Mail To: Secretary, Newwest California Club
P.O. Box 90430, Los Angeles, Ca., 90009

$3.00 per year or special charter subscription: $6.00 for three years, or $25 for lifetime Gold Circle membership.

Membership includes subscription to NEWWEST.

New Member:

Name_____

Street _____

City, State, Zip _____

Enclosed $ _____

FOR AN ENCORE . . .

If you think we've made some blatant omissions in our selections, please send us the name of your favorite restaurant. If we use it in what we hope will be our next edition, maybe the chef will give you a free meal. It's worth a try and we'd appreciate it. Just tear out this postcard and drop it in the mail.

Name of Restaurant: _____

Address: _____

Phone #: _____

Type of food served: _____

_____

Price range for dinners: _____

Your favorite dish: _____

_____

Other comments: _____

_____

Your name: _____

Your address: _____

_____

Any comments on the book: _____

_____

CAMARO PUBLISHING COMPANY

P.O. Box 90430

Los Angeles, California

90009